MW00329938

GETTING BACK UP

A STORY OF RESILIENCE, SELF-ACCEPTANCE & SUCCESS

HARMA HARTOUNI

Getting Back Up
A Story of Resilience, Self Acceptance & Success

Copyright ©2021 by Harma Hartouni

Published by
The Harma Group

Hardcover ISBN: 978-1-7362416-0-8
Paperback ISBN: 978-1-7362416-1-5
eISBN: 978-1-7362416-2-2

This book is dedicated to those who have struggled in life and been ashamed of who they are because they are different, to those who have had to find a way to accept where they are and choose where they're about to go.

Contents

Preface

I DECIDED TO WRITE *this memoir because I don't know anyone who has had a life like mine, and I thought it was worthy of being told. Throughout the process, it became much more than just storytelling. I have remembered things that I buried deep. I have thought about things in ways I had never thought about them. I have learned about myself, my culture, and the people around me.*

Before it was finished, I asked a very smart entrepreneur whom I respect and trust to read a few chapters. Afterward, she asked me a question I had not considered. She asked me how I define myself. If someone gave me one single word to describe who I am at my very core, what would that word be? Am I a businessman? Am I a gay man? Am I Middle Eastern? Am I an immigrant? A father? A husband? Am I a self-made man? None of the possibilities she threw at me felt definitive, and I realized the question was far more complicated than I expected it to be.

How do we, as multifaceted humans with a host of diverse experiences, interests, and responsibilities, begin to define who we are in one single word? Not describe but define. It's not easy.

Fortunately, I had a book about myself I could read to help guide my answer. As I read drafts, I started comparing chapters and events. I started asking what the person in one particular chapter had in common with the person in another chapter. What inherent quality was obvious and critical throughout? I realized there was only one part of me that was not only applicable but vital to every single chapter. I am all of the things my friend suggested, but the overarching thing I am is a survivor.

Being a survivor can mean a lot of things. It can mean strength, misfortune, sickness, pain, trauma, resolve, or resilience. For me, it means all of those things, but most of all, it means tenacity. It means I do not give up on what I want. And ultimately, what I want is to be happy and honest. I believe happiness can coexist with the darkest and most challenging pieces of who we are. I have been victimized, but I am not a victim. My past does not in any way dictate what I am capable of in the future.

I believe everyone is a survivor. Everyone can take the things that have happened in their lives and grow from them. Whether you learn from them or just develop a heightened immunity, you can find purpose in life's challenges.

This isn't a biography; it's merely a collection of events in my life that have been the most impactful in leading to where I am today. Everyone has a story. I am telling mine because I want my husband, my colleagues, and my kids to know it is never about what happens to you; it is about what you do with it.

I am using my past to create a better future. I am moving forward.

Introduction

WHENEVER I GOT IN BED as a child, I was never entirely sure what kind of night I would have. Some nights were peaceful and idyllic. I fell asleep, dreamt a dream I wouldn't remember come morning, woke up, and was off to school. Just like so many other children around the world. Other nights were much different. On other nights, I was jolted out of sleep by the crashing and banging of bombs and high-pitched alarms reverberating in my ears. On these nights, there were no dreams—only reality. My parents rushed into the bedroom I shared with my younger brother and sister, yanked us out of bed, and quickly dressed us. Fresh water and clean clothes were packed and ready to go in the hallway—a precaution in case we weren't able to return home. Then, in the dead of night, still bleary-eyed and confused, we ran across the street to the basement of a tall, nondescript building. My parents had to move swiftly. There was typically a maximum of ten minutes after the sirens went off before the bombing began.

It was the 1980s, and my home country of Iran was in the midst of the Iran-Iraq War. We lived in Tehran, the capital of Iran and one of the many cities raided by Iraq. We hid in the basement of the concrete building across the street because if the building was bombed during a raid and collapsed, it was possible we would be able to survive and eventually be rescued. With the sounds of crashing and destruction faintly in the distance, we sat in the dank basement, among the other hundred or so neighbors and families, waiting for the "all clear". When it came, we headed home and back to sleep, ready to resume our ordinary lives. At least, until the next night.

An hour and a half east of Tehran, there was a small area called Bumehen. Bumehen was where many Armenian families owned land and built villas and "garden" (vacation) homes to spend their weekends away from the city. One week during the war, everyone in Tehran was warned in advance that there would be an especially violent raid with more bombing than usual during the upcoming weekend. We were warned to leave the city, if possible, in favor of somewhere less dense until the chaos subsided. Bumehen was the perfect place to escape. Fortunately for us, a friend of my father's owned a vast plot of land there and invited our family and many others to come and ride out the raid.

When we arrived in Bumehen, it was unlike any place I had seen before. The town was mostly untouched land with large parcels of thick, deep green grass with rabbits and birds scurrying around in every direction. It was the polar opposite of the soot and mangled buildings of Tehran. Thirty or forty people were invited to pass the time at our friend's Bumehen home. Despite the serious occasion, we all tried our best to make the most of it.

Still absorbing how different it all was from what I was used to, my eyes zeroed in on a man with a donkey. I am an animal lover and have been since I was a kid. I loved dogs and cats, rabbits, etc. However, my absolute favorite animals were horses. I was enamored by them. They were tall, majestic, and elusive—no one owned one. A donkey isn't quite a horse, but it is horse-adjacent, and it was good enough for me. I begged and begged my father to let me ride it. "Please! Just one ride? Please!" But the answer was no; I was too young, and it was too dangerous. I settled for being a bystander, an observer as one kid after another lived out my greatest fantasy. I watched each one climb onto the donkey, and with a slap of the ass by its owner, they were off. The donkeys knew exactly where to go, and the rides lasted about ten minutes, each one the exact same loop. Even now, as adult, this memory has stayed with me. A random moment in my childhood that somehow left its mark.

Though my father felt I was too young to ride the donkey, I wasn't too young for a different learning opportunity. Still sulking, my father summoned me over to him with a swift snap of his fingers. I walked behind him, quietly, without a clue where we were headed. Eventually, we reached the man who owned the donkey. Maybe my dad had had a change of heart and wanted me to ride after all! Not so much. The donkey owner was also a landowner. I didn't realize it at the time, but my father wanted me with him to see how he made business deals, something he would continue to include me in for many years to come. My uncle joined us.

The four of us continued walking for what seemed like forever through the thick, luxurious patches of kelly-green grass until we finally arrived at what looked like absolutely nothing. Just more grass. My father carried a rope and stakes in his hands. He tied the rope to one of the stakes and buried it into the earth. We all followed behind him like minions, walking around the property, sinking stakes into the ground, slowly defining a perimeter. We continued and crossed a stream that ran across the property and buried more stakes. Before long, he had outlined the three separate parcels of land, two large and one small. The area was beautiful. As an adult, when I think back to the unspoiled richness of the property, it makes me both grateful to have experienced it and disappointed my children will never have an opportunity to see it as I did. Today it looks quite different: the trees have since been cut down, and the lush green expanses have been replaced with large plots of dirt, lifeless in comparison to what it once was.

My uncle and father each took a piece of paper and created *sanad*, similar to a deed in Iran, to take them to the county to make them official. It was then, during the weekend of a raid, that we purchased the land for what would eventually become my family's very own garden house.

I can still remember the look on my father's face as he made the deal, a self-satisfying smirk that said, *Look at what I am capable of.* It was a moment of pride for him and perhaps a jolt to his ego as well. Sometimes, when I do well in my business and things go just right, I catch myself with a similar smirk. It is gratifying to be reminded of what you can do. There are so many traits my father could have passed down to me, some good and some not so good. But this one, I appreciated. He was the type to never boast about himself but to let other people take notice of his achievements and do the talking for him.

Over time, my father and uncle developed the land, building walls to separate their lots. They built a house and pool and planted fruit trees. We had peaches, plums, apricots, sour cherries, regular cherries, walnuts, and red and green apples. It was Armenian in every way. And by that, I mean Armenians love fruit trees. We plant them wherever we go, whether its Bumehen or Glendale. It's not home unless there's a fruit tree. Between the trees, they also planted eggplants, tomatoes, mint, and cabbage. On another part of the land, we raised chickens and roosters. The chickens produced so many eggs that we could give individual family members twenty eggs each and still have extras. I guess you could say we were eating organic before it was the "in" thing.

Our garden house was a source of pride for our father. He relished the opportunities to go there on weekends to entertain friends and family. For us, going to the garden house was a chore at best and a nightmare at worst. Every time we went there, I became overwrought with anxiety. We were the first to build a home there, but eventually, we were surrounded by other beautiful villas. Those villas had the types of luxuries you think of in a home away from home—multiple bedrooms, plumbing—but our garden house was a bit different. We had only one bedroom, but we also had the most land of anyone around. In America, square footage is a status symbol. In Iran, it's land. The modernity of our garden home was far less important than the land upon which it stood. Especially to my father. Plus, it was important to him that his children not be spoiled or lazy. A one-bedroom garden house on an expansive piece of land was just enough to show others he was a man of means but not so much that we got too comfortable.

Each weekend, when we drove up to the garden house, the first thing I had to do was unload the car, careful not to scuff the walls of the house with everything. I then checked on all the trees and chickens. After that, it was time to clean the pool. If you are envisioning a young boy wading through crystal clear, aqua-colored water with a large pool net, go ahead and take that thought and throw it away. Our pool lacked one fundamental feature that makes cleaning far more enjoyable—a filter. Each weekend when we arrived at the garden house, the pool was deep green, filled with the week's algae, animal waste, leaves, and awful insects.

I'm sure you have been in a pool before; it most likely had a filter. Have you ever thought about how you clean a pool that doesn't have a filter? Probably not, so I am going to give you a play-by-play on how it went down at our place.

With a hose, I drained the pool so that the murky green water drained directly back into the land. As the pool was draining, I waded through, submerged with only tarantulas and other insects brave enough to keep me company. I would often ask my father if, this time, I could wait until the pool was empty before I started scrubbing. But the answer was always no. Time was of the essence. The sooner the pool was scrubbed, the sooner it could be refilled with clean water and the sooner we could take a dip. So into the green water I went. Every once in a while, I squealed in disgust—big mistake. Any effort to appeal to my father failed and was generally met with insults like "faggot" or "girl" (an insult in the hypermasculine culture of Iran).

To make the task at hand even more challenging, he not only wanted the pool as clean as possible, but he also wanted me to use the water as it slowly drained out of the pool to clean the walls. I took large wooden brushes, dipped them into bleach and then into the water, and scrubbed away. My father's instructions were clear: don't scrub too hard or the paint will come off, but make sure all the algae is gone. It was a task to find the right amount of pressure to ensure a crystal-clean pool without any hint of scraped paint. It was also important not to get bleach in the water, because the water was simultaneously being drained into the ground and bleach would harm the trees. Every cleaning session took anywhere from two to three hours, depending upon how dirty it had become since the last. When I finished, two things were always true: the pool was pristine, and I was exhausted.

But the job wasn't done just yet. I filled the pool with cold water from our well. Then, finally, voila, we had a swimming pool to enjoy! And enjoy it we must. Our dad insisted we all jump in. There was no rest for the weary or the murky, nasty water-soaked. The last thing I wanted was to swim in ice-cold water. It wasn't up for discussion. There was a pool—you swim.

Looking back, I am grateful for the chore of cleaning the pool every weekend. It sucked. But it taught me that sometimes you just have to suck it up and do what you need to do to move on. Sometimes those things are thankless and met with expectations when they should be met with gratitude and appreciation. But as I've learned in business, when you do a great job, people may reward you, and they very well may not. You have to be proud of what you put into it regardless of whether others realize it.

Our garden house would come to be an immensely important backdrop for much of my adolescence. But when I was scrubbing away, what it represented most was my father. Each wall represented his tenacity. Each tree, his pride. Each detail, his resolve to have things his way or no way at all. In fact, my memories of the garden house are almost as complicated as those of my father. I am stronger, better, smarter because of the time I spent there. I have fond memories and sad memories. I loved it, and at times, I hated it. With green pastures, red cherry trees, and blue skies, my memories of the garden house are far from black and white, and the same can be said for my relationship with my dad. The garden house was the perfect example of my father's traits. His desire to win.

◇◇◇

When my father purchased the land for our garden house, he made a concerted effort to buy the largest parcel he could find. He didn't make any luxurious improvements to it. The house he built there was modest in comparison to some of the other homes in the area. Instead, he spent the money on the land. When it came time to sell, he made more than other owners because he had the most tangible asset. It was a sacrifice, but he thought long term. I do, as well. If you want to be successful, you must think long term, and you can't insert comfort into the equation. You must continue to build, sacrifice, and invest in your dreams if you want them to come to fruition. No one gets rich fast. You can find comfort fast, but wealth is built slowly with patience and diligence.

◇◇◇

My mother and father are both Orthodox Armenian, and they met in Iran. My mother was one of five children: four daughters and one son. My maternal grandfather was a chauffeur for the US embassy in Iran. During the Iran hostage crisis, he shuttled American hostages from the embassy to the airport to escape Iran. After the Iranian Revolution ended, in a show of gratitude, my mother's entire family were given green cards so that they could relocate to the US. Over a few months, my mother's family sold all of their possessions and prepared to emigrate from Iran to the United States. Shortly before they left, my mother's family went to church for Easter service. Holidays are significant in

Armenian culture. They provide an opportunity for us to let loose, come together, and spend a day where the ultimate goal is fellowship and celebration. In an intensely religious and conservative culture, Easter is probably the most important holiday of the year. It was made even more significant because, as Armenians, we were seldom permitted to embrace or enjoy our Christianity openly in the Muslim state of Iran. That day, after church services, the Armenian community, including my mother and father, gathered.

In Armenian culture, Easter means eggs. Well, I guess that is the case for a lot of cultures. Specifically, in Armenian culture, Easter means playing "Eggs," a traditional game passed down from generation to generation. To play, each participant grabs multicolored eggs that have been prepared for the occasion and finds a partner; you want to find the most substantial, heartiest-looking egg in the batch. Once you've matched up, you grip your egg with your entire hand to give the egg the most support possible. Your partner will then use his egg to hit the bottom of your egg and then the top. His goal is to crack the shell; your goal is not to let that happen. If your egg survives getting hit at both ends without a crack, you and your partner switch positions. The person whose egg doesn't crack moves on to a new partner. After moving from person to person and collecting eggs, the person left with the most at the end of the game wins.

My seventeen-year-old mother sat with her sisters, enjoying the festivities, when my twenty-eight-year-old father approached her for a game of Eggs. In Iran, it's not taboo or inappropriate for a twenty-eight-year-old to approach a seventeen-year-old. As they played, they casually flirted and got to know one another. After the game was done, my father asked my mom out on a date, and she accepted.

During their first date, they fell for each other. I imagine if I were to go back to that evening and interview my mother afterward, she'd surely be smitten and might even say it was love at first sight. Though she has never shared any details about their first date, she eventually revealed to me that they were so enamored with each other that they were intimate. That *was* taboo in Iran. Unfortunately, their union was seemingly star-crossed. My mother's family had green cards, and that was an opportunity none of them intended to pass up. Shortly after that Easter, my mother moved with her family to Los Angeles.

My father was one of three children: two boys and one girl. His life was much different than my mother's. He was a child of divorce many times over. His father was married three times, and his mother was married twice. When he was only twelve, his mother passed away after she had remarried. His stepfather viewed him as nothing but a burden, a child who was not his and he was stuck caring for. He took it out on my father with his fists.

To make matters worse, his parents had never planned to have a third child; he was a mistake and, as a result, almost two decades younger than his siblings. His family was poor and absent. He relied on his friends as family and never really experienced love until he met my mother.

It wasn't long after my mother had relocated to LA that she and my father began corresponding and having brief but loving phone calls. At that time, calling internationally from Iran was a chore. My father would find a public phone, prepay, call my mother, and they could speak for a maximum of three minutes before being cut off.

To him, the effort was a show of love. Look at what great lengths he was going just to speak to her! Nonetheless, the gallantry quickly faded. Wrecked with longing and not one for long-distance relationships, on one of their calls, my father gave my mother an ultimatum. She would either come back home to Iran, or he would tell everyone in the community she was not a virgin.

You must understand the gravity of my father's threat. In Armenian culture, being a sexually active and unwed woman means you will be considered a whore. Period. Sexual experiences for women can be only with their husbands after they are married. Premarital sex brings shame to both the woman and her family. In fact, a woman who was no longer a virgin was not seen as someone worthy of marriage. If people found out, she would likely be resigned to being single for the rest of her life. Because the Armenian community was so small, even from thousands of miles away in America, the fear of being ostracized by her community was too much for my mother to bear. She relented. She convinced her parents to let her move back to Iran to be with my father, and she got married two weeks later. None of her family were there. After the wedding, they moved in with my father's older sister in what would become a dysfunctional living arrangement. My mother and my aunt never saw eye to eye, and often, my aunt was emotionally and physically abusive toward her. The jealousy of having a younger woman in the house who was beautiful and came from a higher social standing—and had moved from America—made it impossible for my aunt to give my mother a chance.

When my mother agreed to move to Iran to marry my father, it was under the understanding that they would move back to the US as soon as possible. After all, they could have a better life in America, and my mother had a close and supportive family there, unlike my father's family in Iran. But when the time came to prepare to move back to America, my father decided he didn't want to. He didn't want to leave his family, even though my mother had left hers. He didn't want to be in a new country he didn't know, and he didn't want to have to learn a new language. He didn't want to be alone. To make matters more complicated, my mother was pregnant with me.

After finding an obstetrician my father approved of, my mother explained to the doctor privately that she had a green card. The doctor told my mother she should seize the opportunity and go back to America. He agreed to help her. He told my father that there were complications with the pregnancy and they should make every effort to ensure she had the baby in the US. At seven and a half months pregnant, my father agreed to allow my mother to travel back to America by herself. And by agreed, I do mean he gave her permission. In Iran, a married woman could not leave the country without the permission of her husband. She flew to Austria to renew her green card since it had expired. She stayed with strangers and was completely unable to speak the language. There, she obtained a visa that would permit her back into the US, where she would be able to get her green card renewed. Eventually, she made it and shortly after gave birth to me.

Dad and me.

After I was born, and with each passing day, my father's distrust of my mother grew and grew. He assumed she had run away and was either having an affair or simply had no intention of returning to him. Each time they spoke, he insisted that she return to Iran as soon as possible. Simultaneously, she and her father tried to appeal to him to join them in California. Finally, after much persuading, he agreed. Because he couldn't get a US visa from Iran, he flew to Turkey to get one. He was denied. He went to Austria instead, denied. Italy, denied. Even though his wife had a green card and his son was an American citizen, none of the American embassies would give him a green card. After months of traveling, he went back to Iran. On the surface, he was furious; after all, what about him was not good enough for America? Underneath, I'm sure he felt inferior, especially considering his wife was from a respectable family and had made it to America with relative ease by comparison. My father demanded my mother move back to Iran; any discussion of him moving was closed. So, when I was four and a half months old, my mother journeyed back to Iran, where she and my father settled into their own place. Looking back, the entire ordeal likely only made my father more domineering.

Three years later, my mother was pregnant again. Once again, she traveled to California to have her baby, and once again, my father attempted to come to America to meet her. Once again, he was denied a visa and, in retaliation, ordered my mother to return with my sister and me in tow. When we arrived in Iran, Immigration took our American passports and my mother's green card. Iran no longer allowed dual citizenship, and so if my mother wanted to stay in Iran as a citizen, she would have to relinquish her American citizenship. Knowing my father would never let her return to America, she obliged.

My brother was born shortly after. He is the only child in our family who is Iranian-born. Growing up, my sister and I often joked about how

My brother and sister's christening. I was six years old, my sister was three, and my brother was less than one year old.

we were born in a modern American hospital, and he was born in an Iranian hospital. If we wanted to get under his skin, we called him Khomeini's son. Khomeini is arguably one of the most influential Iranian leaders in modern history. Ironically, Khomeini is somewhat responsible for my brother being born in Iran, as well as the fact that we would not return to America until we were adults. He passed the laws.

◇ ◇ ◇

I didn't choose to be born in an Orthodox Christian family, particularly one living in an intensely Muslim country. I didn't choose to grow up during a war or have a difficult relationship with my father. I didn't choose to be gay.

14

No one chooses the circumstances they are born into. It's luck of the draw. But where and how you are born and raised ultimately plays a major role in who you become as a person.

Nonetheless, this is my story and how I came to be. Growing up during the Iran-Iraq War taught me that if you go through major life-changing events and setbacks, you have to learn to bounce back and move forward. When we heard the bombs every night, we had no choice but to wake up and keep moving forward. There was no time to be afraid or to feel the unfairness of the situation. That is my secret to life, success, and happiness. If you have business troubles, relationship troubles, family troubles, whatever your troubles may be, you can't get stuck or wallow in them. Successful people learn to either fix or adapt to changing circumstances in the interest of pressing on.

1. The Bathtub

You are never powerless, even when others overpower you.
You can take back your power and find strength
in trauma, no matter how long it takes.

WHEN I WAS SEVEN, on the last day of school before the summer break, my mom and dad picked me up from school together. Immediately my inner alarm bells went off. My parents rarely picked me up from school together. On top of that, my one-year-old brother was sitting in the backseat. As we drove away, I realized that we were taking an unfamiliar route. We were not on our way home. Where were we going to? As much as I wanted to know, I was smart enough to know not to ask.

After driving through the city for some time, we arrived at a narrow desolate street in front of a dark and nondescript office. The four of us entered and sat in a small and dimly lit reception area with only four chairs. It looked similar to a doctor's office, but there was something off about it. You know when you go somewhere, and it just seems a little bit sketchy, but you can't put your finger on why? This place was like that. There was one door in the entire room with no sign or indication of where it led. When you're seven, your life is all about routine. This unexpected change in mine, particularly one so creepy, deserved an explanation.

Not long after sitting, my father stood up, took my brother's hand, and walked through the mystery door. I sat in the waiting room with my mom, completely silent and completely confused. The silence suddenly broke as my brother began screaming as I had never heard before. They were stunning, bloodcurdling screams. Keep in mind, my brother was only one year old, and at that age, screaming is routine. This was not that kind of screaming. This was not the cry of a hungry or tired baby but something much worse. Shortly after, my father came back, grabbed my hand, and led me beyond the door.

My knees were weak with fear, and I so desperately wanted to rip his hand off of mine, turn around, and run as fast and far away as I possibly could. I still had no idea what awaited me beyond that door, but I knew it was terrible. As we cleared the threshold, I looked around what was an incredibly sparse examination room. There was little more than a lamp, a chair, and a bed with straps attached to it. My father removed my pants and underwear. A man came in. I know now that he was a doctor, but you would not have been able to tell by his clothes or his demeanor. He tied me to the bed. I always think of doctors as having quiet confidence about them that helps put their patients at ease. They also typically explain what is going on. But this doctor was completely silent; he had no intention of putting me at ease or assuring me that everything was going to be OK.

In his right hand, he held a large syringe. With his left hand, he took my penis and drove the needle into it, injecting me with some sort of medicine. There, as I laid on the bed, fully cognizant of everything that was going on around me but too young to understand any of it, I was circumcised. My mother, who always felt the pain of her children acutely, sobbed softly in the waiting room, providing the only soundtrack throughout the entire ordeal. In contrast, my father was stoic (save for a few grins of pride). He felt what he was having done to me was both his fatherly duty and in my best interest. When it was over, the doctor stitched up my penis and gave my parents strict instructions that they were to return to his office in two weeks to have the stitches removed. I was in agony. I remember the pain vividly.

About a week later, I overheard my parents arguing in another room. My father screamed, "No, let's just do it here!" I could not make out my mother's responses, but based on the tone of her crying, she vehemently disagreed. It did not matter. A few moments later, my father appeared in my doorway, grabbed my brother and me, and led us to the bathroom. The bathroom was an unremarkable, large square room with powder blue tiles and a white porcelain bathtub. My brother and I stood behind him as he filled the tub with water. I began to breathe heavily; my heart began to palpitate. I was not sure what he had planned, but my intuition told me that I should be afraid. I started to cry but quickly collected myself as best as I could because I knew if I cried, I would get a beating. My father stripped us both and put us into the tub. There was just enough of the warm water to cover me up to my waist. My brother sat in front of me. My father knelt so that his knees were both squarely in front of the tub. He was impervious to how confused and afraid I was of the situation and him.

After our circumcisions, the doctor had bandaged our penises to protect the stitches and facilitate healing. As with most bandages on an open wound, after a few days, it became hard and was fused to the skin. As soon as we were in the bathtub, my father took his large hands, reached in, and ripped the bandages off with one quick motion. That is when the blood started. After the bandages were off, with one hand holding my penis, my father took a pair of scissors in his other hand and cut my stitches. Then with his index finger and thumb, he removed each stitch one by one, as if he were removing pins from a pincushion. Any average human, let alone a child, would scream and wail in agony if someone were ripping stitches from their genitals. Even then, in so much pain, tears ran down my face as I summoned all of my strength to remain silent in the hopes that I could spare myself a beating. I am not sure whether my father even realized we were crying; he refused to look at us. When he finished, the bathtub looked like a scene from a horror film, our blood having turned the water a deep, translucent red color.

Afterward, my father collected my brother and me from the tub and put us back in our room. He was never one to console. By his standards, his fatherly duties were complete. He could resume whatever else he had planned for the evening. Fortunately, my mother was always there to pick up the slack. She rushed into our room with a tub of petroleum jelly in her hand and covered our wounds. They eventually healed.

So many years later, my views on this event are complex. I am honestly grateful that my parents had me circumcised. That being said, the way that I was circumcised . . . left much to be desired. It was traumatic. It was gruesome. It was something I could never fathom doing to my son. I have three children, all born via surrogate. I'm no stranger to the miracle of childbirth and what women's bodies go through to bring new life into this world. I will go out on a limb and say I think most men feel fortunate not to have to experience it firsthand. I do not know what having a baby feels like, but I can say, after having stitches ripped out of my penis, that has to be somewhat in the zone.

◇ ◇ ◇

It may surprise some, but my circumcision is an experience that I look back on frequently when I am faced with a tough decision or have to summon the strength for something. As a child, you have no choice or power in any of your circumstances. And yet, it still falls on you to make peace with what happens to you and move on. It's not fair, but it is the reality. So how do you move on from the trauma? And more importantly, how do you reframe trauma so that you gain strength from it? I often think, If I can make it through having stitches ripped from my penis in a bathtub with no anesthesia, I can afford to take a chance. The outcome can't be any worse than that. *Dark? Perhaps. But it's the only way I can think of the pain with acceptance and purpose. If you have experienced trauma, consider what power you can extract from it. Isolate that power and use it as strength.*

2. The Factory

Sometimes strength lies in accepting abuse
to protect the ones you love from it.

My FATHER WAS ALWAYS a very hard worker. It is yet another quality I am grateful he instilled in me. He was not necessarily the most brilliant man in the room, but he was willing to work for everything that he had. When I was growing up, alcohol was illegal in Iran. Predictably, bootlegging booze was a thriving underground industry and a great way to make a living. Despite the penalty of a monetary fine, whipping, and jail time, my father decided to try his hand at it to help make ends meet for his family.

During the same time, he also worked as an assistant at a factory where they made metal molds. They took raw steel, heated it, and molded it to the desired size. My father's job was to sand the steel down to create the mold that plastic would eventually be poured into. It had to be incredibly precise, so he had to sand with his fingers. I specify fingers, not hands. This wasn't like a carpenter sanding a large piece of wood by hand. This was sanding a piece of steel to exact proportions with incredible detail. That was the only way to ensure whatever plastic was poured in and molded was the same for every piece. Even now, I am impressed that he had the will to get up every day before dawn and do a job that so many would consider tedious.

With the money he made, my father eventually purchased machines and leased a small space outside of town where he would start his very first business. The last time my mother returned from visiting her family in the United States, she brought frames and molds with her for various women's hair ornaments like barrettes and hair clips. After the revolution, women now wore full hijabs in public. The desire to ornament their hair, in their own time, behind closed doors, grew exponentially. Products like barrettes were a hot commodity. My father capitalized on this and, with the frames my mother brought, started manufacturing barrettes.

At first, they were able to make only white pieces. But my mother came up with the brilliant idea of submerging the pieces in large pots of boiling water and adding vinegar. This allowed them to be colored—like eggs. Afterward, the plastic barrettes were put into bags, stapled, and sold at the local bazaars. It was a successful business, and shortly after, my father also began to make plastic glass and pitcher sets. Again, in Iran, the changing social landscape provided the opportunity to manufacture products that may not have been as desirable in earlier times. Because of the war, crystal and glassware were costly and not attainable for many. By creating high-quality plastic sets that were crystal clear and looked as close to real glass as possible, my father was once again able to tap into a healthy, burgeoning market.

Eventually, my father leased another factory space closer to town. It was located in the basement of a building. Here, he was able to hire a staff to help him expand his operations. He employed both men and women. They were all Armenian. Men were in charge of the more taxing manual jobs, such as handling large pots of boiling water, adding color to plastics, and carrying heavy objects. For the women, the work was decidedly more mundane. They would clock in, sit in a room, and assemble the barrettes. After quality checking, they'd test them and then package them. Once they were in boxes, the men would put them in storage.

When I was eleven years old, my dad hired another employee for the factory—me. Just like in the US, students in Iran are out of school for break during the summer. That summer, my father came into my room in the wee hours of the morning. I was asleep on the bottom bunk of the bed I shared with my younger brother. Bleary-eyed, he pulled me out of bed and yelled, "Get up, you lazy ass. You have to work." I had no clue what he was talking about. But I did what I was told.

Though I was working for my father, we didn't go to work together. Instead, I took a taxi, or rather, I took taxis. There was no Uber or Uber-equivalent in Iran. The luxury of being able to hail one taxi to take me exactly where I needed to go was not one I was privy to. In fact, taxis operated more like a cross between a city bus and an Uber Pool. To get to work, I went onto the street and waited for a taxi drive by and pick me up. Each taxi held five people (six including the driver): three in the backseat and two in the front. The taxi drove in a general direction toward where the group was headed, but it stopped wherever it stopped. After getting out of one taxi, I walked to another street to try and hail another taxi that was going even closer to where I was headed. From taxi to taxi, one direction to the next, eventually I ended up close enough to walk the final distance to my destination. That first morning, I took five taxis to get to my father's factory just outside of town. I had to report to work by seven fifteen.

That morning and every morning after that, I was responsible for opening the factory. Other employees who arrived earlier than me usually waited in front of the large metal doors, anxious to get inside and start their day. I handed out time cards to the employees, which were their tickets in. On the first day, after checking everyone in, I turned to close the door behind me and saw my dad sitting in his car, watching. I don't think he followed me during the entirety of my journey to work, but he made sure I was there on time and got the job done.

When I worked at my father's factory, I always avoided the men and hung out with the women. They were nicest to me, and I felt most comfortable with them. At my father's factory, there was a small room with a bed, desk, and bathroom. Often when my father was there, he and a female employee would disappear into the room alone and reemerge some time later. I noticed that he treated her vastly better than the other female employees. I didn't ask questions. After all, I may have only been eleven, but I wasn't an idiot. I knew what he was doing, but at that age, I hadn't figured out it was wrong. The culture was such that men could do whatever they wanted. My father was a man and only doing what men do, with a don't-ask-don't-tell mindset—it was never questioned.

In many ways, my father's factory was an extension of his masculinity and autonomy. He ran the show, he made the rules, and he could do whatever he wanted there. As I got older, I started to become even more aware of his indiscretions and how they manifested themselves in our home life, particularly in his relationship with my mother. Always abusive, he was especially so when most men would otherwise feel guilty. It was commonplace for my father to accuse my mother of infidelity or interest in other men shortly after he had had a rendezvous with an employee. Usually, his accusations would progress to violence, and he would beat her. Oddly, even as I got older, it still wasn't his infidelity that upset me. However jaded it seems, in my view, every man was unfaithful. What I took issue with were the mind games. He victimized my mother in retaliation for his own transgressions. Seeing the pattern and having a full view of how those violent episodes were prompted was what ultimately gave rise to my anger toward him. A feeling that would never entirely subside.

On one particularly horrific evening, my father came home from the factory. I got back at the same time via taxi. He and my mother got into an argument in the kitchen, as they so often did. I don't recall the subject of the fight. My mother attempted walking to a different room to diffuse the situation, but my father screamed at her to sit down. As he hurled insults and obscenities her way, he reached for a ceramic teapot. He struck her with it. He hit her over and over again with the teapot until it broke across her body, the ceramic pieces flying everywhere. My father left her there, lying on the floor, crying. She couldn't walk for days. To this day, I refuse to have a ceramic teapot in my home. It's too hard to shake the memory.

One of the most challenging parts about being a kid living in an abusive household is the feeling of helplessness. I wanted to save my mother. I wanted to intervene and tell my father if he took one more step, raised his hand one more time, he would have to answer to me. But that was impossible. If I intervened, it would only make it worse. The only people I could protect were my younger siblings from seeing what I had seen so many times.

◇◇◇

My father's burgeoning success was a powerful lesson for me. He put everything he had into his business. Often people see only the result of a successful business but don't know how much sacrifice went into building it. My father sacrificed. When others might have been tempted to take the fruits of their labor when they first had a taste of success, he invested and reinvested in himself. Instead of buying a nice car, he purchased a better truck that would allow him to grow his delivery operation. He took his products to the bazaars and markets to sell them himself. He shopped around for the best deals on plastics and materials. Back then, there was no Instagram or Facebook. There were no overnight successes or marketing miracles. To make it, he had to be shrewd and diligent. He operated under the philosophy that it wasn't how much you made but how much you kept. He taught me things that are built fast fail fast but things that are built slowly and with intent are generally built for the long haul.

It was a valuable lesson I have used in building my own business but with a few caveats. I don't use my success as a way of dominating the people around me, especially my loved ones. My business isn't a pass for me to do whatever I want. I also, unlike my father, value loyalty and recognize it as a two-way street. Now that I have my own business, it is so important to me that I am not my sole focus. I want the people around me to grow and thrive, because it inspires dedication and ownership.

3. My Grandparents

If you change the way you look at things,
the things you look at will change.

WHEN MY GRANDPARENTS LEFT IRAN, they had no intention of ever coming back. They were US citizens and focused on building a new, peaceful life in the US. But they also never expected their daughter to move back to Iran and raise her family there. If they wanted to see their daughter and grandkids, they had no choice but to return. And return they did, when I was in middle school. It wasn't going to be our first meeting; after all, they were there when I was born.

Nonetheless, it would be our first memorable meeting. As I anticipated their trip, I was both excited and curious. My parents' dynamic and home life had been solidified at this point. He was an abusive philanderer, and she was a trapped woman resigned to spending her life with a man she had long stopped loving. But, as with every constant, all it takes is a new variable to change the outcome. I found myself wondering how my grandparents' presence would impact the way my father interacted with my mother, my siblings, and me. Would he be on his best behavior, or would he assert his dominance as head of the household in the toxic way he often did?

Throughout her marriage, my mother always kept the negative aspects of it as private as she could; she seldom shared them with her parents. Or anyone for that matter. Even so, my grandfather, in

particular, had fantastic intuition. He knew they were far from blissfully happy. My mother was also a daddy's girl. Her "choice" to move
to Iran and marry my father without any family present was heartbreaking for him. Nonetheless, at that point, the marriage had taken
place well over ten years prior, and it was time to reconnect as a family.

My grandparents arrived and stayed with us in our home. My
father decided that in honor of their visit, we would make *ashe mast*, a
traditional Iranian soup made with a yogurt base. He bought a ton of
yogurt from a random man in the village, brought it home, and told
my mom to make the soup. Wary of the quality of the yogurt, my
mother pushed back. She didn't want to make ashe mast with random
street yogurt and have us all get sick. She had a point, but questioning
my father was a bad idea. She unwittingly pushed one of his biggest
buttons, his insecurity about their class differences. Why wouldn't
yogurt from the village be good enough to eat for her and her parents?
He was from the town; was he not good enough? Just like that, a fight
quickly ensued. My grandparents looked on as my father screamed at
my mother, cursing her and making sure she realized that regardless
of whether her parents were present, she could never speak to him in
such a way. He then ordered her to make the soup. He left our home
and returned a short time later with exponentially more yogurt. She
wasn't just going to have to make one pot of soup; he ordered her to
make as much soup as the amount of yogurt he'd purchased would
allow. Nearly forty bowls worth. Crying, she made the soup, embarrassed by what her parents had just seen. Even though forty bowls of a
dairy-based soup was a ridiculous amount that even a restaurant would
have trouble getting rid of, we dare not throw any of it away. His reaction to my mother's unwillingness to make it in the first place got us
into this mess. We were all afraid of what his response might be if we
discarded even a drop of it.

Over the next few days, we ate soup for breakfast, lunch, and dinner.
My grandmother was so disgusted, she left and went to stay with her

sister for a few days. My grandfather even woke up early in the morn-
ings when he thought no one else was awake and heated three or four
bowls just for himself. It was the only way that he could show support
and solidarity for my mother. Heartbreakingly, even amid abuse, it was
not culturally acceptable for my grandfather to speak up or out against
my father. He'd given my mother away, and she was no longer his to
protect. To object or bring it up at all would make everything worse.
My father's anger was so significant, it was almost like another person
living in the house. It was something to steer clear of. Something to not
agitate—or else. If you've ever heard the term "Don't poke the bear,"
living with my father's anger was kind of like that. Except in his case,
the bear liked being poked because it provided an opportunity to show
you just how ferocious it could be.

For the rest of my grandparents' visit, my father behaved as he
always behaved. He was a brute. He managed to fight and argue with
my mother every single day. In fact, during the visit, my father took the
opportunity to involve my grandparents in his fights with my mother.
He recounted false and exaggerated stories to convince them of how
terrible of a wife my mother was. He also made it very clear to them
that if she were not obedient, he would divorce her. This was his trump
card. Indeed, it was the trump card of many Iranian men. Threatening
to divorce a woman was like threatening to cut off her oxygen supply.
In a country where misogyny, patriarchy, and sexism were not only
prominent but codified into law, a divorce was the easiest way to leave
a woman destitute. A divorced woman was considered a pariah, a slut,
a woman who was unfit for a legitimate place in society.

Though his motives were deplorable, his method was effective.
Threatening to divorce not only sent chills up my mother's spine (as it
had the many times he had threatened it before), but it also sent chills
up the spines of my grandparents. While the sight of their daughter emotionally and physically abused by her husband must have been
unbearable, the idea of what her life would become if she were divorced

was simply unthinkable. She would not have been permitted to retain custody of her children. There were no circumstances under which a woman could maintain custody or any agency over her children unless the man agreed. Even if my father had murdered someone and been thrown in prison, he would retain rights over his kids. In that country, and that culture, at that time, it was better to be the wife of an abuser than an ex-wife. Knowing my mother, I think she would have been strong enough to handle being called a slut, but losing her kids (particularly to her abusive husband) was not an option. My father knew this was the best way to ensure no one would speak up on behalf of my mother or challenge him in any way. He had asserted his dominance, and damn if he wasn't good at it in the absolute worst way.

When the trip was over and my grandparents left, I could only assume they were relieved to be out of our house and away from my father. That was the first and last time I ever saw my grandfather. He died a few years later of cancer, only months after his other daughter's (my mother's sister) untimely passing. My father did not permit my mother to attend his funeral in the US. After the deaths of my grandfather and aunt, while on the phone with my mother, my grandmother lamented how she wished so desperately that it had been my father who died instead of her husband and daughter.

◇ ◇ ◇

Looking back, it's hard to think about that time with any positive lens. The way my mother was treated by my father was abhorrent. The fact that a group of adults who witnessed the abuse all felt powerless to do anything about it only makes it more heartbreaking. It wasn't as if my mother was hiding her abuse. My father was taunting her; he was flexing. He knew there was nothing anyone could do to challenge him.

So instead of a lesson, perhaps some levity? A silver lining, if you will. I can say, unequivocally, that my mom now makes the absolute best ashe mast that you will ever taste in your life. I guess when you have to do something over and over again, even something that you hate, you start to get good at it. I suppose that is a lesson for business as well. I've always made a concerted effort to practice and practice at everything I take on while shutting out whatever negativity might be surrounding me. I firmly believe that if you keep working on something, eventually you will become an expert at it. My mom became an expert at making ashe mast. She also became an expert on doing whatever she felt she needed to do to protect her kids. That was, perhaps, her biggest success.

4. The Motorcycle Ride

As a boy, how do you explain an attraction
to men when you're not gay?

I WENT TO ARMENIAN MIDDLE SCHOOL. Going to an Armenian school in Iran was pretty different than going to a religiously affiliated school in America. For example, an American Catholic school simply blends standard education with Catholic teachings. But in Iran, we were subject to the regulations put in place by the Muslim state. Even though all the students were Armenian, we weren't allowed to learn our language or anything about our culture. Everything we learned was in Farsi. All of our teachers were Muslim except for one older Armenian teacher. He was round with a thick white beard and, ironically, as the only Christian teacher in the place, he looked a lot like Santa Claus. Every morning we got in line and sang the national anthem of Iran and then did a very brief prayer from the Christian Bible. After that, everything switched back to Farsi, and school began.

After school, either practicing gymnastics or dance—I can't remember which.

The school was an old historic building, likely built when shahs were still in power. It was completely divided in half—one side for boys and the other side for girls. There were two separate entrances, so if a parent had boy and girl children, they had to do two drop-offs. The playground was divided by a large metal fence and covered so you couldn't see from one side to the other, except the covering had fallen away in one small corner. Even though this sounds very different than American middle school, we still were typical preteens in a lot of ways. We dated and passed notes to each other. The missing part of the fence covering was a godsend for facilitating romances between boys and girls. The only difference between boyfriends and girlfriends at my middle school was that they likely never saw one another's face. Not just because we were kept separate but also because all the girls were required to wear hijabs. I've never fully understood why the girls needed to wear hijabs when women ran the entire school.

In an environment like the one I grew up in, in which hyper-masculinity is commonplace, it isn't difficult to spot an outlier. I was an outlier. In school, I already stuck out among the other boys. People often complimented me on my looks. Teachers and other adults gave me preferential treatment for reasons unbeknownst to me. As my parents began to make more money, our clothes and shoes reflected our elevated financial status. Not to mention the gifts my grandparents sent from the US. Because I stuck out and also did not fit in with the other boys my age, I was bullied. I was called a "faggot" and "woman" by my peers all the time. As I walked down the halls, boys took their elbows and knocked me against my head as I passed by them. I didn't retaliate. Over time, the abuse became so frequent that I, like most children in that position, sought ways to avoid it. In middle school, recess was my time to escape. While all the other students went outside to play and socialize, I started staying inside to savor the short amount of time when I didn't have to worry about anyone bullying me. As I am sure a lot of other gay men would agree, as an adolescent, bathrooms were often the most uncomfortable places. Second, perhaps, only to locker rooms. So I thought ahead. The best way to avoid a bad situation was to go to the bathroom when absolutely no one would be there.

After recess, the bell rang, and all of the students headed back to class. I knew that with a class just starting, the bathrooms would be empty—the perfect opportunity for a bathroom break without having to worry about being accosted by other boys.

It was also during middle school that I started a period of sexual awakening—or to put it more simply, puberty was on the horizon. Sometimes I wonder whether, in some twisted way, the homophobic bullying I endured was responsible in part for my sexual revelations during my middle school years. I never really knew what "gay" was. It didn't outwardly exist in Iranian culture, and I had never (to my knowledge) encountered or seen a gay person. There were straight men, straight women, and what we now refer to as transgender women. Those were the categories. Those were the people you saw in Iran. As I got older, I learned men did have sex with other men, but it still wasn't considered "gay" sex. If two men had sex, the "top" (the man who dominates the other man) was still considered a man. The "bottom" (the man who was dominated) was considered a "faggot." Being a faggot was deemed to be akin to being a freak. I also knew a lot less about sex than I imagine the average American boy of the same age might have known, especially as it related to my attractions.

As a boy, I was seldom allowed to interact with the opposite sex. Even at church, there were efforts made to keep boys and girls apart. Whenever I did interact with girls, it was typically on holiday or for some special occasion. The setup begs the question: If you are never around girls, what opportunity do you have to realize you are less interested in them than boys?

Sex was never discussed. Rather than sex or attraction, the real barometer for being different was masculinity (or the lack thereof). Perhaps everyone's constant talk of what they perceived to be a distinct lack of masculinity in me made it easier for me to look within myself and see I *was* different. I guess middle school kids have a reliable gaydar. In any event, I did start to become more aware of my attractions. I still wasn't at a point where I knew (or could admit to myself) what it all meant, but I started to develop crushes. I began to notice my most attractive male teachers and fantasize about them during the school day. I noticed men's bodies. Their calves and legs, the hair on their arms, their eyes—they all stood out to me like exclamation points on a page.

It was during this time I got the sense that a friend of mine who lived in our neighborhood was in a similar situation. I can't put my finger on what exactly it was about him that stuck out to me or made me think he might also have an attraction to men, but we seemed to gravitate toward each other as friends. We often hung out after school. He was an only child, and his father frequently traveled for work. One day, when his mother was out and his father was on a business trip, we went back to his house after school.

He asked me, quite directly, if I was attracted to men. I didn't fully understand the question, and I don't know what it was about the situation that made me feel so comfortable, but I didn't hesitate to answer yes. He then revealed to me, unsurprisingly so, that he also was attracted to men. It was the first time I had ever admitted that to anyone, and what followed was an open conversation about what it meant to have these kinds of feelings. Eventually, our conversation led to a kiss. The kiss felt like the Fourth of July, like fireworks. The experience of touching another boy's lips was exhilarating.

Nonetheless, the idea that this made me gay never entered my mind. We were simply two boys fooling around and experimenting. Something more common than you'd think. In my experience, when you take boys in the height of puberty and give them no access to girls, they are bound to turn to one another. That was the only time we ever kissed. Even though the experience was significant, I was not attracted to him. He was just a boy and nonthreatening. The type of people who drew my attention were more masculine. I often thought about my geography teacher's body. He was tall and lean, handsome with green eyes. One of the youngest teachers at the school, he had a way about him I found intoxicating. He was easygoing and fun; he made his class fun. He was unlike any other man I had ever met. A far cry from my father and men of his type. Maybe he was my first *real* crush.

At the age of thirteen, the assistant principal at my school offered to give me a ride home. I don't remember why I needed a ride; perhaps I had an afterschool project, as I often did. He was younger than other administrators at the school. He drove a motorcycle. He was *cool.* I sat in front of him, his arms wrapped around my body so he could steer. He asked me to sit in front of him on the bike and then wrapped his legs around mine. From my perspective, this felt innocent. Even though we were quite close, if you've ever ridden on a motorcycle with someone, it requires a certain level of intimacy that simply can't be avoided. But as we rode, I quickly started to feel nervous and strange at the same time. Here I was sitting on a motorcycle in what was the most provocative situation I had ever been in, to date—a thirteen-year-old boy. This wasn't a kiss from the a boy next door, and it was a situation that was hard to comprehend.

The roads in Tehran are chaotic, and there are few traffic laws. This all added to the danger of the experience. I felt he was protecting me. Protecting me in a way a man had not protected me before. And then I felt him being aroused as he sat behind me, and I froze and sat quietly in front of him all the way home. When I got home, both of my parents were outside. Immediately fear and dread washed over me. Would they be able to tell something weird happened just by looking at me? My father had a look on his face as if he had an inkling. But *had* anything happened? I was even more confused.

Afterward, anytime I saw the assistant principal, I was completely unsure how to approach the situation. Sometimes I would avoid him altogether; other times, I would be overly friendly and smile. As time progressed, I started to feel more comfortable around him and eventually continued to maintain a relationship after that incident. After all, it was his job to make sure all the students went out for recess, and as his friend, I could help him inside the school while everyone else was playing. I would have done absolutely anything to avoid having to go outside during recess. If I had to take one for the team and hang out with someone I now realize to have been a creep, I was willing to do it. Fortunately, nothing sexual ever happened between us.

Though escaping during recess was helpful, I wanted a more permanent solution to all the abuse and bullying I was receiving day in and day out. At the time, I had a friend at school who was seeing a hormone therapist. I got the idea that perhaps a hormone therapist might be able to help me too. I found one not far from my father's office and made an appointment. No one knew but me. I took the last appointment of the day because I did not want to run the risk of anyone I knew seeing me there.

I went after school. It was a small and unmemorable office. No one was there except for a nurse behind the front desk. I told her my mom was on her way but running late so she wouldn't get suspicious or, worse, not let me see the doctor. I sat down, nervously fidgeting for a few moments until the doctor came out and ushered me into his exam room.

"What brings you in today?" the doctor asked.

"I don't want anyone to know I am here. Please don't tell anyone at all I am here."

"OK, son. No need to worry. Why don't you just tell me why you came to see me today?"

"Are you able to give me hormones to make me more manly?" I asked.

"What do you mean?"

"Everyone thinks that I am too feminine. I am terrible at soccer and basketball, and everyone makes fun of me. I love dancing, and people tell me my mannerisms are like a girl's."

"OK, hold one moment for me, please."

The doctor left the room and returned a few moments later with his colleague, another doctor. They instructed me to remove my pants so they could examine me. Then, one of the doctors put his hands on my leg. It was then that I could see both doctors were aroused. They unzipped their pants and started to touch themselves while staring at me the entire time. I was frozen, paralyzed with intimidation, disgust, and fear. I didn't know what to do. Each doctor finished and zipped up their pants and, as if nothing had happened, told me I was perfectly healthy and had nothing to worry about. They assured me I was not feminine and I would be absolutely fine. They basically tried to make me believe what they had just done was an examination.

I left the doctor's office and ran as fast as I possibly could to catch a cab home. It was one of the if not the most disturbing incidents that I have ever experienced.

◇ ◇ ◇

Though I was too young to realize what was going on, the assistant principal was a predator and left the school after that year. I later learned he had done what he did to me, and much worse, to several other students. He was arrested and put in jail for a short time. When it came to light, my mother asked me if he had ever done anything to me. Sometimes I wonder if she asked me in the hopes that I would say yes. Not because she would ever want something terrible to happen to me but because it would give her a reason that she seemed to crave—a reason for my gayness, an explanation. I assured her he had not. Even if he had, and even if she had known when it happened, as an Armenian mother accusing a Muslim man of assaulting an Armenian student, any action she took would have been pointless.

Even now, it is hard to completely fathom I was sexually assaulted as a young teenager by multiple men at different times. Men, I might add, who were meant to be trustworthy. I had never even considered the possibility my doctor or teacher might sexually assault me. Looking back, what I find most sad is I put myself in those situations out of sheer desperation to be like the other boys and not be bullied so much. I know none of it was my fault, but it's difficult not to feel regret.

5. When Dad Is Away

Of all the things a kid could dream for, I dreamt of my parents' divorce, but it was impossible.

MY FATHER OFTEN TRAVELED. Sometimes for weeks at a time. His excuse was always he had to travel for work. To some degree, that was true. He imported and exported goods, and his company was relatively lean, so it made sense he would need to travel. Back then, where we lived, it was extremely uncommon for men to travel for work, particularly to different countries. But at this point, my father was anything but a common businessman. Over the years, he had built a great business for himself. His success gave me a sense of confidence among my peers. Though our relationship was very complicated, I was proud of my father's success.

Pride aside, my father wasn't always traveling for work, and if he was, his trips weren't wholly devoted to work. I am reasonably sure he found time to squeeze in some play. One of the most obvious signs his trips weren't always work-centric was when he traveled over important Armenian holidays like Christmas and Easter. Nobody Armenian worked on Christmas or Easter, so the likelihood he was conducting business on those days was almost nonexistent.

Even though it was pretty much an open secret that my father used his work trips to "work" and engage in whatever other activities he felt he couldn't do in Tehran, we all reveled in his absence. Including my mom. Being the oldest son, when my father was gone, I was in charge of the family. Let me reiterate that I was in charge. And not in some sappy, "man of the house" sort of way. I was actually in charge. Even though she was an adult and fully capable of heading our household when my father wasn't present, the duty fell to me because I was a boy. It's a bit odd to think about now, particularly from an American lens. My mother was never in charge of her own family. But it's something that applies in many cultures: often the firstborn and, in particular, the first son, is the second-in-command when it comes to all things family related. Though incredibly patriarchal, the responsibility helped me and challenged me to become a more mature and thoughtful person. It made me decisive.

Regardless of who was in charge, when my dad left, there was a collective sigh of relief from everyone. It was during those times that we could be ourselves, as opposed to walking on eggshells whenever my father was home. A typical weekend with my father out of town consisted of us heading to the kebab place by our home. We always ordered a big pot of kebab with rice, tomatoes, bell peppers, and meat. We'd take it home and put down the newspaper on the floor and sit around the pot. My mom would fetch plates and greens to eat with the kebab. We'd shake the pot so that the food would be equally covered in the butter and seasoning and then eat it with our hands or bread. Sitting on the floor didn't serve any purpose except for the fact that it was spontaneous, and we got to eat dinner on our terms. If my father had been there, he would have policed what we ate and how we ate it. No salt, no butter, no flavor, everything had to be his way. We wouldn't even be able to stop eating until he had finished. His absence was a treat.

As we ate, we watched TV together. There was only one television channel in Tehran. Around 2:00 p.m., it broadcasted cartoons. At 4:00 p.m., it would play an adult-geared movie but never with subject matter dealing with love, romance, or sex. Those kinds of films were censored in Iran. At that time, no one had their own private VHS players, so if you wanted to see a movie, it had to be one shown on TV.

When my father was away, our house was peaceful. We got to be normal kids, and the constant tension in our average day-to-day was replaced with ease and joy. Whenever my father returned, it was as if someone had turned off the electricity and all the life and excitement instantly drained out of our home as we resumed our usual routine of muddling through the darkness of his temper. Even the smallest things were a *thing* when he was home. We all had to eat more onions and greens with every meal because he thought they were good for us. He

didn't allow any of our food to have salt in it, because he didn't like salt, forcing me to keep a secret stash of salt in my bedroom. Once, during dinner, my dad had a bite of my food and tasted the salt I had snuck out and added to it—that didn't end well, another beating.

My father's fuse was typically the shortest when he returned from a business trip. It was then that he would pick fights with my mom the most. He often accused her of cheating or sleeping around. Though, deep down, the notion that she would ever have the time, ability, or balls to cheat on him was a bit silly. Even so,

I was the ring bearer, and my sister was the flower girl. Somehow my brother missed the memo.

it was during fights like those that I worried the most for my mother. Often when he brought up the idea of her cheating, she felt inclined to do the same. This always kicked things up a notch, and I always worried that they might turn violent. Sometimes, when they fought in the morning, I pretended to go to school and instead hid by the entrance of our building. I waited for the fight to end and my dad to go to work, and then I went up and quietly checked in our apartment to make sure everything was OK. Sometimes I even enlisted the help of neighbors. If I asked neighbors to stop by, it would usually hasten the end of the fight. Though this didn't always work. Some of our neighbors were dealing with the same issues.

Below us, there was a wealthy couple who were very similar to us. The family consisted of three kids, two boys and a girl who were the same age as my siblings and me. There was a great deal of domestic violence in their household as well. It may have been even worse for them. The mother of the family, a beautiful woman, was continuously beaten, and so were the kids. During one fight, she even lost a tooth. After some of their particularly gruesome battles, the husband would leave and go pick up his girlfriend to bring back to their apartment. He proceeded to make out with her in front of his beaten kids and wife as they lay injured on their bed. It was sick stuff. I thought, *Well, my dad isn't that bad*. It was a low bar. At one point, the wife attempted to leave her husband to escape the constant abuse. She was arrested and stripped of her parental rights. My father would often use this as a warning to my mother. "See what happened to her," he'd say. Back home, Iranian law applies to everyone, regardless of your religion. Men always have the final say, regardless of the circumstances. Custody is always awarded to the father, and it's a chief reason why women do not leave their marriages even when they so desperately should.

◇ ◇ ◇

In Tehran, there is a large Armenian community center called Ararat Sports and Culture Complex. It was accessible only to Armenians and, in many ways, was the center of Armenian society and culture in Tehran. Men and women were permitted to interact, and the women didn't have to wear hijabs while they were on the premises. It was where most Armenians gathered to socialize and play sports together.

There were pools, sports fields and courts, stages for productions, and even a church. In a place like Iran, Armenians needed to have a safe space where we could be openly Armenian and embrace our culture and religion.

I played soccer there. I was a goalie, and my hand-eye coordination left a lot to be desired. I would have preferred to spend my afternoons doing pretty much anything else, but my father insisted on soccer—it was his favorite sport. My father didn't come to every game, but when he did, I usually disappointed him. During one game he attended, I played very poorly. I missed catching a ball, and the other team scored. I can't remember if it was my first miss or if I had lost a few at this point. Regardless, my dad was pissed. He stormed down the bleachers and onto the field in the middle of the game! In front of everyone, he grabbed me and threw me off the field. He hurled insults at me: "You're a faggot!" "You're complete shit!" "Get off the field, you woman!" Once I was off the field, he went to the goal and played like me. Literally, against a group of middle school children, my father played goalie while I cried on the sidelines. I'm not sure which was more humiliating, the fact that this happened in front of everyone or that he took my spot in the game. Sometimes I think it was worse to take my place because it made me feel not only humiliated but also inferior. Since then, I hate playing soccer and most organized sports. I do enjoy watching soccer, but it is solely to enjoy looking at the soccer players.

Instead of soccer, I realized I had a passion for dancing. Dancing was illegal in Iran except for at the Armenian community center, so I decided to sign up for a class there. It was overwhelmingly filled with girls. Though historically, men are professional dancers in Armenian culture.

One of the reasons I joined a dance class and stuck with it was because I loved my dance teacher. She seemed to see something in me I did not see myself, and we ended up forging a very strong bond. She was a gifted teacher and taught us traditional Armenian

Dance rehearsals for the end-of-the-year event.

dancing, ballet, and some other dances from different cultures as well. Eventually, her following grew, and as I got older, more boys started signing up for the dance class. Perhaps I started a trend.

I stuck with dancing for years, going five days a week for nearly three hours a day. Diligently working with the same teacher,

More dance rehearsals.

I enhanced my skills and eventually became her teacher's assistant. I think I may have been addicted to dancing. It became my complete passion; it was my escape. I figured being on my toes in class was better than being constantly on my toes and walking on eggshells at home. Eventually, she asked me to help teach a younger class as her teacher's assistant. I was finally good at something. Ironically, my father was extremely supportive.

◇◇◇

I have learned in life you have to be capable of dealing with unexpected situations that are beyond your control. You have to be comfortable with what is uncomfortable. When my father was away, I could be myself. My mother made that time bright and enjoyable. It was truly a respite. But living with my father taught me things are often unpleasant. Sometimes you have to live amid unpleasantness with an intense desire for things to be different. So the question then becomes how you deal with it. If you are in a position where you aren't able to change a situation, don't waste energy questioning it. Use that energy to adapt as best as you can to try and hold on to your sanity. The difference between a human being and a rock falling off a cliff is a rock falls silently and a human screams and wails even though the outcome will be precisely the same. If you are going through a difficult process, don't fight it; see it for what it is and get to the other side. Otherwise, it makes it all the more miserable.

6. Beginning High School

I figured no reputation is better than a bad reputation.

AFTER MIDDLE SCHOOL, I asked my parents to let me go to private school instead of going to the Armenian public school with all my middle school classmates. I was only fourteen, but I wanted a fresh start. After so many years of constant tormenting, I felt like high school was the perfect opportunity to create a different persona. I thought if I went to a new school where I didn't have a reputation, it would take people longer to realize I was more feminine than the other boys. I made a conscious effort to alter how I presented myself. I spoke with a deeper tone, wore larger clothes, I didn't wear colors, I tried to learn basketball, and I even used slang I would have never naturally used. I wanted to create a new reputation for myself in which people viewed me as just another, how do you say . . . dude. When my parents agreed, I had the distinct feeling I was finally going to embark on a new journey and perhaps have a bully-free existence. I was relieved.

In addition to the prospect of having a fresh start, I knew going to private school would improve my career prospects. The private school generally helped students get into better colleges. In Iran, you have to have an idea of what your career goals are long before you go to college. Your desired career path shapes what high school you get into. I wanted to be a doctor. I thrived in math and science and knew it was a respectable profession that my family would be proud of. In our culture, the most respectable professions were doctors, lawyers, or engineers. If you were fortunate enough to work in one of those magical three professions, you could get whoever and whatever you wanted when you eventually decided to marry. Everyone catered to you. Parents of young women were all too excited to give their daughters away to men they knew would bring respect and financial stability to her life. In theory, you didn't have to worry about your daughter if she married a doctor, lawyer, or engineer. For me, it wasn't the prospect of marrying a woman that enticed me toward being a doctor. It came down to two things: (1) I wanted to make money, and being a doctor was lucrative, and (2) I wanted to earn my parents' respect. To me, being a doctor was the perfect path to achieving both of those goals.

My parents were surprisingly hands-off in my search for my high school. I vetted potential schools myself. While doing so, I became friends with a neighbor who was the same age and also looking for a new private high school. We joined forces and ultimately decided on a small, affordable Muslim school on the other side of town. I was reticent to ask my father for the money, but surprisingly, he agreed with no hesitation. I often thought he enjoyed having leverage over me; if he were the one paying for my school, then I was indebted to him. Whatever his motivation was, I was just fortunate I was getting what I wanted. There was one catch: in exchange for allowing me to attend the Muslim school, my father made me promise to go to an Armenian afterschool, where I could continue to learn about Armenian history and culture.

In my new high school, people could tell I was Armenian by my accent. However, I tried my best to downplay my heritage. I wanted to blend in with everyone. I just wanted to feel normal. It was at my new school that I learned Islamic prayer. After listening to the same thing every day, even if you don't know what you're saying, eventually, you'll pick it up.

Though I was at a completely new school, it wasn't long before I started to identify boys who carried themselves differently, looked at me differently; there was just something off. Now I know that "sixth sense" was just my gaydar.

Despite my efforts, it didn't take too long for Harma, the "Dude," to give way to the normal Harma. A gay guy who didn't know he was gay but sensed others who were, too, in his vicinity. And, as to be expected, like any other red-blooded teenager, I started to experiment.

◇ ◇ ◇

No matter where you are in life, if you're dealing with something deeply personal—a secret—and you think the answer is to change your persona and become someone else, I can tell you it is a fool's errand. It is always better to be who you are and to live in acceptance. Find relationships, environments, and jobs that fit who you are. Don't expect to change the inside by changing the outside. You can develop skill sets to change habits and thought patterns, but you cannot change who you are and how you were born—so work from the inside out.

7. Kidnapped

Being in business with someone is like
marrying them—you should always date first.

As I GOT OLDER, my father's business continued to flourish. During
the fall of the Soviet Union, Armenia had become its own country.
On its west side, there was Turkey, with whom Armenia had no
relationship. On its east side was Azerbaijan, with which Armenia
was at war. South of Armenia was Iran. Because of its conflict and
lack of relations with its neighboring countries, the newly independent
Armenia had very little in the way of resources or allies. Opportunities
to improve its infrastructure were also limited. As a result, my father
saw a great deal of opportunity for importing and exporting goods
into the country. He also saw an opportunity to help his people. It
often felt it was somehow easier for him to be compassionate with
others than give that kind of care to his own family.

The very first eighteen-wheeler truck to cross the Iran-Armenia
border was my father's. By this time, he was in the business of
importing two goods. One was portable kerosene heaters, which
were a very hot commodity, as many in Armenia did not have heat
to warm their homes or cook with. He also imported frozen fish.
Fish was not especially popular in Iran, so it was relatively inexpensive to buy. Fish is very popular in Armenian cuisine, so it was a
lucrative import. He eventually imported dried pasta, and ultimately,

he graduated to construction supplies as Armenia's infrastructure became more promising.

Always eager to expand his business, my father decided to try his hand at exporting lightbulbs into Iran. He developed a business relationship with two men in Armenia who owned a lightbulb factory. The two men, who had government connections, were some of the wealthiest Armenians in the country. Their family was also immensely powerful both in legitimate and illegitimate businesses. They were what we would consider in the US to be a crime family.

Although the two brothers were involved in unsavory business practices, my father still trusted them. On the business trip, the brothers convinced my father to invest all his capital into lightbulbs, including the money he had made from his heater and fish imports. They promised high returns, and my father was eager to tap into just a fraction of the immense success the brothers had seen. When the lightbulbs arrived in Iran via truck, the overwhelming majority of them were broken. My father's initial instinct was to assume it had been a mistake. The lightbulbs must have been broken in transit. But ultimately, he came to realize the lightbulbs had boarded the truck that way. He had been duped. The brothers repackaged all of the unusable light bulbs that were unfit for sale from their factory and shipped them to my father, keeping the money he had invested. My father was mortified, not just because of the money he had lost but because he had been so naive to put so much trust into people who were so far from having integrity. Not one to be taken for a ride, he decided to sue the brothers in public court through the Armenian embassy.

Even though he lost a great deal of money on the lightbulb deal, my father continued his import and export business. At this point, it was our family's most significant source of income. On one trip, he invited me to travel with him. Once again, he felt it was a valuable experience for me to see how he made deals. Whenever my father went to Armenia, he rented out a small two-bedroom house to stay in. When I accompanied him, I stayed in one bedroom, and he stayed in the other. The bedrooms shared a door, and you had to go through one room to get to the other. While spending one-on-one time with my father may have been a fantastic opportunity to connect, it was the farthest thing from his mind. Trips to Armenia were for work *and* play. The fact that I was there didn't change that.

One night, while accompanying him on a trip, I woke up in the middle of the night to noises that I had never heard before. I got up and went to the door that was shared with my father's bedroom. I tried opening it, but it was locked from the other side. Once I was closer to the door, it was easier for me to make out the noises I was hearing. My stomach began

My dad and me at dinner on the first night I accompanied him to Armenia.

to turn as I realized I was hearing my father, his friend, and two women having sex in the same room. I'm not sure how best to put into words the level of disgust I felt at that moment. It was sickening. I had long known my father used his trips to Armenia to cheat on my mother. I had made peace with it; that was simply the kind of man he was. This was not that. This was an entirely different monster. My father, a married man who had forced me to come on a business trip with him, was having loud sex in the next room with a woman as his friend had sex with another woman in the same room. He had purposely locked me in my bedroom so I could hear everything but not leave. It was obscene.

The next day, presumably after his friends had left, my father picked a fight with me. I don't remember exactly what started it, but, as he usually did, the battle quickly gave way to him insulting me with slurs and curse words. But this time, our fight was a bit different. Amid his cursing fit, he asked me, "What are you going to do about it, run and tell your mom what happened last night?" I didn't intend to tell my mother. I desperately wanted to never think about it again.

My father had to go back to Iran for a short stint during our trip to Armenia and decided to leave me with our rental home's caretakers. Shortly after he left, a chauffeured car came to the rental house, and the chauffeur told me my father had arranged for me to stay with the wealthy family he had done the lightbulb deal with. At the time, I was completely unaware of the lightbulb deal and that it had gone sour. We had met before, shared meals, and traveled together. I had no cause for concern. I assumed that their intentions were legitimate, so I very willingly went with them. I arrived at their garden home, which was beautiful. They had a housekeeper who cooked for us, horses, fishing, and even a son my age I could spend time with. It was an enjoyable time, and, to be honest, I was happy to be away from my father, especially after what had happened. Even so, after about four days with no contact with my dad or anyone else from my family, I began to get bored and was eager to go back home. I asked my hosts if they knew when my dad was going to return from Iran. Their responses were vague. "Soon, he'll be back soon."

On the fifth day, as I sat alone in my hosts' billiards room, the door swung open. In walked the driver who had brought me there, the son of the family I was staying with, the housekeeper, and my father. I was a bit shocked since I had had no forewarning that he would be returning that day. Brusquely, my father ordered me to gather my things so we could leave immediately. I was beyond confused. I tried asking questions, but all my father said was we needed to go. Once we left, my father explained to me the family I had been staying with were not friends and he was actively suing them. They found out he had left me in Armenia and took the opportunity to send him a message by taking me. I had been kidnapped.

During the time I was (unknowingly) being held against my will, my father had no idea where I was or whether I was still alive. He enlisted the help of his much older brother, who had left Iran as a young man and moved to Armenia. They had only just reconnected on a trip my father made to Armenia a few months before. Initially, they searched throughout the capital, where I had last been seen. Eventually, they found out I had left our rental home in a chauffeured car. From there, they put two and two together and realized I must have been taken by the crime family.

After leaving the garden house, we drove back to the capital so we could board a flight back to Iran the next morning. One of my uncle's daughters decided to come with us. Though we didn't know her well, she was very friendly and took to linking arms with my father as they walked. It was harmless but a bit odd. She was tall, young, and beautiful with striking green eyes and blonde hair. As we stepped off the plane and through the gate, my cousin's arm linked with my father's, and her other hand was holding mine. My worried mother, who never met my father at the airport, was sitting at the gate, nervous with anticipation. The idea I had been kidnapped shook her to her core. When she saw the three of us walking toward her, adding to her emotions was a wave of confusion. Who was that woman? Was this happening? Not only was her son returning from having been kidnapped but her husband was arm-in-arm with a strange and heavily made-up blonde woman she had never met. Given his penchant for cheating, my mother naturally assumed he was bringing home a mistress. It was a one-two punch. She instantly went from being a concerned and distraught parent to a confused lioness, desperate to understand exactly what was going on and what this meant.

◇ ◇ ◇

My father's ill-fated lightbulb deal was a powerful lesson for me. A lot of people can promise a lot of things, but there is value only in what can be delivered. As a businessman, you have to trust the people you go in business with. No business can be successful without strong relationships, and that requires a certain level of vulnerability for a business owner. But you should never enter a business relationship blindly. Albeit morbid, whenever I go into business with someone, I ask myself whether the person I am joining forces with would be a good role model for my children if I were to die tomorrow. If the answer is no, then we are not suited to work together, no matter how enticing the opportunity is.

8. The Konkur State Exam

I worked hard and achieved exactly what I set out to, but I wasn't satisfied because my success wasn't good enough for someone else.

WHEN I WAS EIGHTEEN, I took the Konkur, a college entrance exam every student in Iran is required to take. It's similar to the SAT that college-bound students take in the United States, but it carries a bit more weight. Not to say the SAT is insignificant, but in the US, getting into college is composed of a lot of different factors, not just test scores. In Iran, the Konkur is the ultimate deciding factor for every Iranian student's academic future. An Iranian student's entire academic career leads up to this test. During your high school career, you study within specific tracks that determine your career path. For example, physics leads to engineering, biology leads to medicine, art leads to liberal and performing arts, and math leads to accounting. The test determines where you get to go to college, what you are allowed to study, and, eventually, what you can practice as a professional. Not only that, but your performance on the test also determines the level at which you can perform in that specific industry. If you are interested in pursuing medicine, your score determines whether you can go to college to be a doctor, nurse, or veterinarian. The test is insanely rigorous, and so, to prepare students for the test, Iranian schools are also very rigorous. The test is all of your education wrapped up into one exam. If, god forbid, you take the test and do not do well enough to place in a college at all, you can't go to college unless you improve your score.

All students across Iran who are preparing to graduate take the test on the same day at the same time. After I took the exam, it took a few weeks before the results came back, which were then published in the newspaper. There was no privacy; everyone's name, as clear as day, was listed along with their score and what it meant for their college acceptance and career path. The results came back in the middle of Ramadan, the Muslim period of fasting that lasts for the entire month. In Iran, during Ramadan, the whole country more or less shuts down. I was delighted with my results and, surprisingly, the first person I wanted to share them with was my father.

I rushed to his office, which was now in the heart of Tehran. Completely enclosed in glass and overlooking the city, my dad's office was a testament to the success he had found as an exporter and businessman. When I got there, he was in a meeting. Usually, I waited, but this was as worthy a time as any to interrupt. I knocked as I simultaneously opened the door. Rushing in with excitement, I proclaimed, "Look who got into university!" With a blank and unimpressed stare, he said: "OK . . . why didn't you knock before interrupting my meeting?" He then asked me to leave.

The entire interaction lasted no more than thirty seconds, but it was a significant turning point in our relationship. My hard work and dedication to my studies had all led up to this moment. This was one of the biggest moments of my life. I wasn't expecting my dad to throw his papers into the air in elation, jump for joy, and take me out for ice cream. But I thought, maybe, for this sort of achievement he might express some happiness or pride for me. Thinking back, maybe I built up that moment in my head without thinking about our relationship and his limitations realistically. Was it realistic to think my father would finally give me some validation? The validation I had so desperately craved for my entire life? I wasn't a good enough soccer player for him. I thought being the first person in my family to get into college would finally be enough. It didn't matter to me that he hadn't cheered me on or supported me. I just wanted the pat on the back. I wanted some affirmation. But that isn't what I got. And it forever changed our relationship. For the better, if you can believe it. At that moment, as quickly as his dismissal, my determination to make my father proud washed away. I no longer cared about school. I didn't care about where I got into or impressing my dad or bringing honor to our family. I was mentally and emotionally checking out of our dysfunctional dynamic.

Knowing our education system in Iran required us to choose our professional track at such a young age had a very profound impact on me. It taught me to start thinking ahead toward longer-range goals. It required me to think about each piece that fits within a puzzle of whatever vision I created for my future. It necessitated focus and a clear delineation between the efforts I put in and the results of those efforts. Going to school to figure out yourself or what you were going to do with your life just wasn't a part of our culture.

It's much different than here in the US, where people seem to struggle more with finding their purpose and what they want to do with their lives. That isn't to say either situation is entirely good or bad. Having to decide at a young age about the rest of your life is an enormous amount of pressure. And that's not even considering the possibility you may choose wrong or decide to dedicate yourself to something you hate. On the flip side, struggling to make a decision and work toward a clear goal can result in complacency or falling behind the curve. I never dreamt of being a real estate broker when I was envisioning my career as a student. But I did learn about cause and effect. Effort and achievement. When I did decide real estate was the right career path for me, envisioning my success was easier because I wasn't overwhelmed or daunted by what it might take. I took comfort in my belief that if you can envision something and then map out how to get there, it's likely you will.

The other valuable thing my schooling taught me was to follow through. Back then, we had no choice. If you took the Konkur test and placed high enough to be a doctor, come hell or high water, you were going to be a doctor. It was not acceptable to give up or take someone else's spot just to toss it away. In my profession, I have learned the value of following through and making good on every promise. I always under-promise and over-deliver. It ensures people's expectations are always exceeded.

9. The Dance Competition

Dancing was not allowed in Iran, but somehow with a little help from a priest and a nun, we danced the night away.

THE COLLEGE I GOT INTO was about an hour and a half from our home in Tehran in a very small town. As soon as I was accepted, I knew I would commute from my parent's home. I was used to Tehran. I had made friends in Tehran. I knew that if I commuted, I would be able to maintain some of the close friendships I had made with people who genuinely liked and accepted me. I did not want to have to make entirely new friends and be in that weird position of feeling unsure of whether strangers could tell I was different. The school was close enough to home that, if I commuted, I could still maintain those friendships even if it meant only seeing them during the weekends. My father never bought me my own car, but he did allow me to borrow his Paykan whenever I needed it. A Paykan is a very popular inexpensive car in Iran. He was out of town frequently and owned other cars, so the arrangement was pretty painless. It offered me even more freedom to be independent, make decisions for myself, and come and go as I pleased.

Commuting from college also meant I could continue to dance. At the time, I had a very serious girlfriend who was also a dancer. She was Armenian and one of the most beautiful girls in our community. She came from a highly respected family, and they were good friends with my parents. On paper, we were a great match, one that could lead to marriage eventually.

One of the things my girlfriend and I connected on was our love of dancing. We were known as two of the best dancers in our community. We decided to create a dance competition at a local church as a fundraiser. Competitors were allowed to perform any style of dance they wanted, and my dance teacher, the nuns, and the priest were among the judges.

Hoping to impress, I knew as soon as we organized the competition that my girlfriend and I would perform a version of Michael Flatley's *Riverdance* as a couple. At the time, *Riverdance* was an international sensation, and I knew if we nailed it, we would win first place. We decided to leave out the tap component and focus heavily on the leg movement. The key to the dance was synchronicity and strength. Every kick, thrust, and jump had to be perfectly timed between the two of us. My legs had to be strong enough to lift her throughout the performance. The competition was planned months in advance. Over those five months, we taught ourselves everything. We watched the *Riverdance* video so many times I could hear bagpipes in my head each night as I closed my eyes.

Around the same time, I started a habit of driving to an older part of Tehran that people I knew seldom went to. There was an old church there, where elderly people who didn't have families lived. Sort of like an orphanage but for old people. I'm not sure why, but there was something about that church and the people who lived there that resonated with me—people without the security and connection that family is meant to promise. There was a bazaar on the way that I often stopped at to pick up lavash bread and pastries to give away at the church. A resident, an old woman, became fond of me, and she and I started spending time together whenever I visited. She knew how to read coffee cups. Reading coffee cups is a popular ritual in Iran, and it's similar to reading tea leaves. After drinking coffee out of a white china cup, you flip the cup so it is upside down on its saucer. Afterward, you lift the cup, and the impressions left by the coffee residue reveal aspects of your future. I didn't necessarily believe in it, but even if you don't completely believe in fortune-telling, it doesn't mean it isn't interesting to hear. More importantly, she enjoyed doing it, and I enjoyed brightening her day. I knew she had no one else.

Five months later, the day of the competition had finally arrived. Our performance was, without a doubt, the best performance I have ever given in my life. We moved with such ease, precision, and strength. It was passionate and intoxicating. Perfect execution of so many hours of preparation. The entire Armenian community was there, cheering us on as we moved in perfect tandem with each other. People were amazed that our bodies—our legs— could move like that. It was a proud day. We won.

Our dance group was invited to perform at a private wedding, and I got to perform a solo traditional Armenian dance.

◇ ◇ ◇

The act of winning lasted about three minutes max (which is kind of a long time when you consider Oscar speeches are only forty-five seconds). It flew by. Yet the work that went into winning took months, hundreds of hours of work, and years of prior practice. There is nothing that happens overnight that isn't tied to some form of luck. Winning the lottery—that's based on luck. Anything based on skill requires preparation. As a businessman, I have learned there is no such thing as an overnight success. Absolutely nothing. Even if it looks that way from the outside. Things always happen gradually, gradually, gradually, and then . . . suddenly.

10. The Last Garden House Trip

I was crushed by my crush's rejection. Yet, twenty years later,
I don't even remember his name.

THE DAY AFTER THE COMPETITION, still riding the high of winning, I went to the church to pay my respects, spread some goodwill, and bring some bread to the residents. As usual, I went to the old woman's room, but she wasn't there. Her belongings were gone, and her room had been completely cleaned. It was if she had never been there. Since she had no family who would have picked her up or moved her, I knew she must have passed away. Feeling the fantastic high of just winning our dance competition coupled with the odd feeling of grief for a woman's death, someone I barely knew, made me feel like I needed a getaway.

Throughout this entire summer, while practicing with my girlfriend for the dance competition and making periodic trips to the church, I also struck up a friendship with a handsome guy who lived nearby. Whenever we looked at each other, our eyes lingered a bit too long. Whenever we spoke, there was a warmth between us that didn't seem entirely appropriate. Deep down, I knew he was like me, though I still didn't know what that meant exactly. Whatever it was, we never addressed it. Not discussing it made it easier to maintain the friendship and made the tension between us safe. Acknowledging it would make it real. When I decided to get away the day after the competition, I knew I wanted it to be with him.

I picked him up in my dad's Paykan, and we drove to my family's garden house and had a decidedly platonic evening. We prepared kebab on the grill outside, drank a little, talked, and then went to bed. Nonetheless, to spend an entire evening with my crush, albeit a platonic evening, was exhilarating. Who knew what might happen during the rest of our time together? The next day, I woke up excited to spend the day with him. There was no sense in us rushing back anywhere. I hoped we could spend a few days at the house uninterrupted. I was surprised and angered when he asked me to drive him to his parents' garden house about fifteen minutes north. But it was one of those situations when you are let down because of your own expectations.

Well, let's unpack that. Now, I can look back at the situation and say I was upset because I had a crush on him. I thought he had a crush on me, and I assumed we both wanted to spend as much time alone as possible. However, at that time, when the concept of having a crush on another boy was foreign to me, I had no reason to be upset that he wanted to head up to his parents' place. But I was. Even then, there was a great deal of compartmentalization when it came to my attraction to men. My desire to spend more time with another boy, perhaps even fool around with him, was so deep and discrete that when the possibility was no longer on the table, I wasn't able to process my disappointment for what it truly was. I just felt anger and sadness. And, not willing to show that anger and sadness, I agreed to drive him where he wanted to go. We jumped in the Paykan and headed north.

I drove to the main road that connects all the small towns with Tehran. It is a small two-lane road with one lane going in each direction. The road straddles the side of a mountain and is coiled like a snake. It was the type of road you might envision James Bond speeding on in a convertible Aston Martin with the top down, with some gorgeous coastal European city as the backdrop. On one side of the road is the mountain and on the other is a cliff. With so many twists and turns, there is not much visibility; you typically can only drive a few feet before there is another sharp turn with no way of knowing what lies beyond it. However, that doesn't stop people from driving as if they are on the autobahn. In Iran, speed limits and road safety were more like suggestions than rules. In fact, nobody really wore seatbelts there, including me. On a road like this, people drove at their own risk, relying on their memory and experience to make up for their lack of caution. The road was not for the faint of heart, but like everyone else, I had driven it many times before and had grown used to its unpredictability. We reached his parents' house and said our awkward and somewhat cold goodbyes.

Still upset our getaway had ended so abruptly, I left his house and turned back onto the main road. I decided I would head back to Tehran. What good was hanging out at the garden house by myself? As I drove back down the mountain, something happened. Now, before I tell you, you should know I am not a religious person. I respect religion, and I am spiritual. I believe there is an order to the universe and things happen for a reason. But growing up in such an intensely religious environment, as a minority who did not practice that religion, I have seen firsthand how deeply rules and beliefs that are not universally held can harm those who do not follow those practices. Put simply: I am spiritual but not religious. Despite my lack of religion, I had what some might consider a religious experience.

11. The Accident

An omen saved my life.

As I DROVE DOWN the winding road, an old man appeared in the passenger seat next to me. He was illuminated, and he had a prominent beard. I was completely in shock, trying to make sense of what I was seeing while keeping my eyes on the road. He raised his left hand and put it on my right shoulder. Looking straight into my eyes, he said calmly, "Do you know that you are going to die soon?" I was in complete shock. Everything about what was happening felt 100 percent real. I couldn't be hallucinating and operating a vehicle at the same time. It truly felt as if a man were sitting in the car with me. And then, just like that, he was gone. I quickly pulled over on the side of the mountain; I needed to process what had just happened. As I carefully pulled over, I positioned my car so drivers from both directions could see me from far away. I took a few minutes and then decided it was time to get home. But, before I pulled away, I thought it might be as good as a time as any to break out that seatbelt. Unfortunately, I had no clue where it was. Fumbling, I found it deep between the seat and the door, still in a black mesh casing. It had never been used. I had never seen anyone wear a seatbelt before in my life, but I was determined to put it on. I fumbled for nearly twenty minutes, trying to adjust it before finally succeeding and pulling back onto the road.

My dad's Paykan was a stick shift. I don't know if you've ever driven a stick shift, but to shift to second gear, you have to speed up. So I sped up. Before I was able to shift to second gear, I felt my car start to drift toward the edge of the mountain. I tried to correct and turn the wheels back toward the road. I had driven this car so many times and never experienced this. There was no rain, and the roads weren't slick. I could not figure out why this was happening. It happened again, and I corrected again. The third time it happened, I saw a large bus coming in the opposite direction.

It was Ashura Tasu'a, a culminating day in the month of Muharram— one of if not the most significant holy months in the Muslim faith. It is a day of mourning and remembrance of the death of Mohammad's grandson. Muslims take to the streets to march together, pray, cry, scream, and pay their respects. They also self-flagellate. A ritual of hitting oneself with chains, swords, or palms to acknowledge the pain and suffering Mohammad's grandson endured. The bus that was passing was taking dozens of people to pray in observance of Ashura Tasu'a.

My car continued to drift, and I didn't know how to stop it. I tried to turn the car as best as possible to avoid being hit by the bus. I worried if my car collided with the bus, I would be pushed off of the mountain entirely. We were so high up, you couldn't see the valley below. If the bus hit me and pushed me off, there was zero chance I would survive. I turned my wheel just enough to avoid being ejected from the mountain. Everything else happened in an instant.

When I opened my eyes, the front of the bus was the very first thing I saw. We had hit head-on. Everything was dead silent as I tried making sense of what had just happened. My immediate first thought wasn't getting to safety or crying out. It was simply coming to the realization I was alive. Quickly, though, the reality of the situation set in and I realized I needed to get out of that Paykan.

I tried opening the driver's door but realized the car was just shy of the edge of the road. If I got out on that side, I would have nowhere to go but off the cliff. I wasn't able to open the passenger door either. The accident had pushed the front wheel of the car into the interior of the cabin, and I was pinned into my seat by my ribs. I didn't feel any pain, perhaps because of the adrenaline. But even today, one side of my ribs stick out, and the other side is inverted.

The only option I had was to flip over the seat into the back of the car and get out of the back passenger side door. Thank goodness, I had strong and flexible legs from my dance training. As I emerged from the car, two men in front of the bus looked down at me in shock. It was the bus driver and his assistant. I'm sure they thought I was dead or, at the very least, not able to move. Seeing the small gold cross hanging from my neck, the two men got out of the bus and started hurling insults at me. They knew I was Armenian because I wasn't wearing black and was not participating in the religious activities of the day. I spoke with an accent and wore gold jewelry, which was a dead giveaway in Iran of someone who was not Muslim. They called me *sag armeni*, which translates loosely to "filthy Armenian, dirty as a dog." Among Muslims, particularly in Iran, dogs were considered unclean. You would never see a dog in someone's home or as a pet. That just doesn't happen, so calling someone was a dog an insult. The insult was very uncharacteristic of what I had experienced with Muslims in Armenia and certainly not a reflection of the overarching sentiment toward Armenians. But in this instance, specifically with these religious men, I was filth. Their hatred toward me, after such a traumatic accident, made me fearful of what might happen next. I was not prepared for a physical altercation. We also were in a pretty remote area, made more so because most people weren't on the roads because of Ashura Tasu'a.

At this point, my car and the bus were still attached. The men were unsure whether they would be able to separate them and, if so, whether their bus would be able to drive. While they worried about that, I worried about my dad. Actually, "worry" is an understatement. I was scared shitless. Possibly more scared than I was about being ejected from the mountain in the first place. I mean, that wouldn't have been ideal, but at least I wouldn't have had to deal with my father's anger when he found out I'd totaled our car. I decided to give the two men from the bus some time to figure out how to get the vehicles apart. Racking my brain, I leaned my back against the side of the car to try to figure out my story.

With my mind going a mile a minute, contemplating how exactly I would explain this to my dad, I heard the driver yell, "WATCH OUT!" I had no time to react. I had no time even to figure out what I was supposed to watch out for. Almost immediately, from behind, I felt a weight like I had never felt before.

The car swerved as it hit the driver. Then it hit me and then swerved and hit the driver's assistant, who was standing just a few feet away. At that point, my body was pinned between the car and the bus with my butt against my car. My two legs were crushed between the bus and the car that hit me. I collapsed onto the road, completely flat.

Have you ever seen a movie where, in a moment of complete and utter chaos, everything on the screen abruptly starts moving in slow motion? That's pretty accurate. In the few moments after I was hit, everything felt surreal. There was no rush of adrenaline. No immediate fear at the prospect of my mortality. I didn't scream. I didn't cry. All I did was collapse. I didn't even feel my head hit the hard pavement. I didn't feel anything; I couldn't hear anything either.

As I looked up, I saw the passengers on the bus busting out of its windows and jumping down to try and get to us to help. I felt liquid running down my neck. I thought it was rain, but as I turned my head upward, I realized it was the blood of the driver's assistant pouring down the road. Like the snap of a hypnotist's fingers, the blood on my neck brought me out of my haze. I needed to get up. I needed to know what the hell had just happened. I tried standing. I couldn't. I looked down and realized my feet were facing backward at almost 180 degrees. My jeans were completely torn. My right leg was covered in blood, and, through the denim, I could see my bone marrow jutting out. It was gruesome. Even so, even though I could see my legs had been mutilated, I still had no pain. Ironically, as I write this, my legs are tingling all over.

As I lay there on the asphalt, completely immobile, the driver of the car that hit us got out and walked toward me. He knelt and put his hand on my shoulder. He said, "It's an Ashura Tasu'a day. Husayn and Hassan will heal you. Don't worry." That was the last anyone has ever seen of him. He left the car at the scene of the accident and disappeared. We later found out the car belonged to the government and was part of the former President Rafsanjani's fleet. In the following months, as my family tried to find the man the car had been assigned to so he could be held accountable, there was never any record of him. The home he had lived in was vacant. His name turned up no records. He, quite literally, vanished.

It took about thirty minutes for any help to arrive. Back then, in Iran, there were no cell phones and no immediate ways of alerting anyone an accident had happened. Since each involved car was inoperable and all the individuals who could drive were too hurt to do so, it became a matter of waiting. Eventually, a bus carrying children down the mountain passed and saw the mayhem and offered to help. They pulled me and the bus driver and the driver's assistant onto their bus. It was then that I noticed the bus driver also had a badly broken leg. The driver's assistant was completely unresponsive. I later found out he was already dead. They put the driver's assistant in the very back row of the bus. They put the other driver on the floor of the bus, and they laid me down on another seat close by. Leaving everything else behind, the bus began to make the descent down the mountain to Tehran for help.

Riding down the mountain, the pain still hadn't hit me. I was just confused about where we were going. I gave one of the adults my father's number and asked them to call him once we reached a phone. I am sure I was going in and out of consciousness.

Laying on the bus seat, I could see out the windows, but my vantage points allowed me to see only enough to make out where we were. I couldn't see the ground, but I could tell we were heading into Tehran. When we reached the city limits, we were met with yet another challenge. Many of the roads were blocked off for Ashura Tasu'a, and those that weren't were filled with mourners marching. I couldn't see them, but I could see the tops of chains moving in unison, almost robotically, hitting mourners on their backs as they self-flagellated. During Ashura Tasu'a, there was no emergency more important than this ritual. Our bus couldn't honk its horn to ask mourners to clear the way. We couldn't call for help at all. We had to move with the crowd at a walking pace. And not just an average walking pace—a mourner's walking pace. The pace at which large groups of people march in commemoration. Each whip of a chain punctuated the painstaking second after second after second as we drove toward a destination I still didn't know. We moved so slowly; I had no concept of time at all. I couldn't tell you whether it was an hour, two hours, or three hours. The only way I could begin to measure it was by the number of times I saw the tops of the chains.

I was raised Orthodox Christian and had lots of Muslim friends. I wouldn't call myself religious. I don't subscribe to any particular religion. But I think it is essential for everyone to believe in something. Even if that something is just to believe in the good in others or the idea that what you put into the world, you get back. Many people don't believe someone appeared in my car and warned me about what was about to happen to me. I don't necessarily expect them to. But it did happen. And whether people believe it or not, what it taught me was to trust my instincts. It taught me to believe in energy and intuition. Whatever it was that came to me that day, an omen, a vision, a warning—I don't know what you want to call it. But it served a purpose in that it showed me things don't just happen. There are rhyme and reason to the

world, and instincts can be the factor that saves you when there is nothing else. My instincts have shaped many aspects of my career, and I've learned, both through successes and failures, to never go against my gut feeling. To always lean into what feels right and to walk away from any situation that feels wrong or unhealthy.

12. The Hospital

I came very close to being part pig.

FINALLY, WE REACHED OUR DESTINATION. We were at the public hospital. In Iran, there are both public and private hospitals, with private hospitals offering better care for significantly more money. The hospital attendants jumped onto the bus and put me on a scoop stretcher (the kind without wheels) and pulled the two bus drivers and me out of the bus. As they carried me off, I could see my father; we must have pulled off and called him on the way with the number I gave. I don't remember. A wave of fear washed over me. Similar to how I felt just before I was hit. I knew that my father was going to be enraged at everything that had happened. Not only had I totaled our car, but I'd also gotten myself hurt in the process. I prepared for him to beat me.

As we got closer, I could see his eyes and his expression. It wasn't one of anger. It was one of fear. A fear I had never seen in him in my life. One of the attendants carrying my stretcher tripped on the stairs leading out of the bus and hit my leg. I didn't feel a thing, but my father and everyone outside of the bus screamed in horror. Out of the bus, the attendants walked in the opposite direction of the hospital doors toward an ambulance and then loaded me into the back. My father must have made arrangements in advance; we were headed to the private hospital. At that moment, as I was gravely injured and still unsure of the extent of my injuries, I felt for the first time that my father loved me.

When we got to the private hospital, my mother was waiting outside for the ambulance, along with about fifteen of our family friends. As they carried me out of the ambulance, my mother came to me, choking on her tears, struggling to catch her breath. I took her hand and said, "I'm sorry about the car." As soon as we made it inside, the attendants rushed me to a private room and sprang into action. I was still not able to feel anything as they cut off my pants. Then they took a large wooden stake with two ends, one for my calves and the other for my toes, and stretched my broken legs so they could be set straight and then wrapped in bandages. They then took three separate stakes, one each for the sides and backs of my legs, and wrapped them around once again to keep them straight. Then they tied my hands to the bed. Yes, you read that right—they tied my hands to the bed.

In the time that my father learned of my accident and arranged for me to be transported to a private hospital, he also researched orthopedic surgeons. He found a young doctor who was considered the best orthopedic surgeon in all of Iran. He wanted this doctor to perform my surgeries. During Ashura Tasu'a, many nonreligious people leave town and go to their garden homes to escape the upheaval. The surgeon just happened to be one of them. Making matters more complicated, in Iran, the ER doctors don't make any decisions about a patient's medication until the patient's doctor has provided instructions. Because my father had identified this surgeon as my doctor and the surgeon was out of town, the ER would not give me any medication. They tied my hands down to the bed to control me when the pain eventually intensified. As my pain started, I started screaming and screaming. I would scream, pass out from the pain, wake up, and start screaming again. The sheer sound and sight of my agony were too much for my mother, and even she passed out. This went on all night until about noon the next day, almost twenty-four hours after my accident, when the surgeon arrived.

Even though I was an adult, my father took charge of my medical care. He paid a family member to travel to the north of Iran to offer the surgeon money to come back and help in Tehran. I wasn't privy to any of the conversations that took place between my surgeon and my father. I had no idea what my treatment plan or prognosis was. In retrospect, that was for the best. My surgeon told my father he was unsure whether I would ever be able to walk again. Both legs and ankles were broken. There was no way of knowing the extent of my nerve damage and whether they would repair. Both my fibula and tibia were shattered, along with both ankles, and my tendons were completely ripped. The injuries were so severe that the surgeon initially thought he would have to perform the surgery in stages, operating on one leg first and then the other a week later. The difficulty in delaying surgery for one leg was that it increased the likelihood of infection significantly. The operation required specific pins that would be inserted into my bones to help facilitate healing. The hospital didn't have them; they had to be ordered and shipped, and this delayed surgery for an additional two days.

Finally, after repeated delays, the time came for my surgery. As I was wheeled into the operating room, I looked at my father, who was walking alongside the stretcher. I said to him, "I am going to die on the operating table, and you never let me see the United States." In a rare show of affection, he took my hand and said, "When you walk again, I promise I will send you to see the US."

Contrary to what he thought, the doctor was able to operate on both of my legs and ankles at the same time. It took a total of eleven hours. Because some of my bones had been crushed in the accident, the surgeon had to trim bones from my hips and put them in my legs to level them off. This was the only way to ensure my legs would be even and I wouldn't have a limp. I was discharged a few days after my surgery, and I went home to begin a very long road to recovery.

I was fortunate. In a lot of cases, pig bones are used as a type of bone substitute. It's ironic, given that pigs are not considered clean animals in the Muslim faith. It's interesting that pig bones are still used to put people back together.

◇◇◇

Working with the best can make or break you. In my case, quite literally. I had one of the best doctors in the world. And I am so grateful to him. Multiple doctors who have examined me and seen my X-rays since, including those in the US, have told me it is a miracle I can walk, and I owe it all to my surgeon. No matter your profession, the people you work with and go into business with can be determinants of your success. I can walk, swim, and jog, and I have a healthy life because my father fought to find the best doctor for me.

13. Recovery

I'll never know whether it was the donkey oil
or the chicken feet that helped me walk again.

THIS ISN'T A SELF-HELP BOOK, but I think a little assignment is in order. Tomorrow when you wake up in the morning, don't move. Don't grab your phone, don't check your email, don't turn on the news. You may be late, you may need to get your day started, but I'd like you to just lie there for fifteen minutes. By the time you reach fifteen minutes, if you can make it that long, I can guarantee you will be going insane with boredom. That is the best way I can describe the nine months following my surgery (minus the pain).

I wore casts from just above my knees down to my feet. At first, they were white, but eventually, and per my request, they were changed to fluorescent green. My parents prepared a bed in the living room for me to recover on. From my bed, I had a view of the outside, and I could see the roof of the house across the street. Throughout my recovery, they demolished the house, cleared the land, and built a new home. When they finished, I still couldn't walk. I slept alone, though sometimes our bichon frise dog jumped on the bed and lay at my feet. Perhaps he knew that was the part of my body that needed the most attention.

Me at our garden house. I was giving my dog a haircut, one of the few activities I looked forward to.

Every eighteen-year-old's dream.

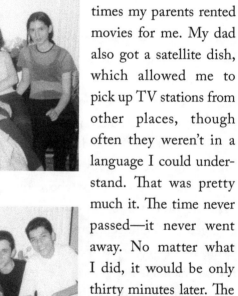

Celebrating my birthday with friends, an uneven cake, and matching T-shirt and casts.

Next to my bed was a bucket that I was able to shift my body enough to pee in. Every morning when I woke up, my mom prepared breakfast for me. My mood was utterly unpredictable, and it didn't take long for depression to set in.

Sometimes I'd scream at her if she didn't prepare what I wanted. When it came time for bathing, my mom put a plastic tarp down beneath me for sponge baths. I felt disgusting and dirty. There was no cable, but sometimes my parents rented movies for me. My dad also got a satellite dish, which allowed me to pick up TV stations from other places, though often they weren't in a language I could understand. That was pretty much it. The time never passed—it never went away. No matter what I did, it would be only thirty minutes later. The highlights of my day were eating lunch, eating dinner, and going to bed. The doctor recommended I eat smaller, healthier portions. My mother lifted me every day and rubbed my back because lying straight without being able to move would create dark blue bruises all over my back. On occasion, my dad rubbed my back, too, but that always felt a bit uncomfortable. We lived on the third floor; getting me up and down the stairs was such a task, I left the apartment only a few times during my entire recovery, for surgery and doctor appointments.

I was angrier than I had ever been. I was also embarrassed. I hated everyone. People came to see me, and I would have to ask them to leave the room so I could pee or shit in my bed in private. It was humiliating. I hated people for visiting me. I hated them because they could walk and I couldn't. I also hated it when people didn't visit me. I hated it when people didn't acknowledge or ask what happened to me. I hated it when people asked me what happened to me. I hated them because they had never cared about me until my accident. I hated the fact that I knew, deep down, people were talking about me behind my back.

There was such an outpouring of sympathy from friends and family, and it started to make me feel paranoid. I didn't feel there was any hope, optimism, or positivity accompanying everyone's sympathy. Everyone just felt sorry for me in a way that made me feel hopeless. Over time, the absence of those sentiments made me feel less like the accident had been a setback and more like it had been a tragedy, one with permanent consequences. Slowly, I started to realize nobody thought I would ever walk again.

It was during this time that I decided I would never live my life in a way that made me feel as though the future was inevitable. Up to then, I had spent my life focusing on two things, school and building friendships. I got into college and had my future laid out for me. I was focused on building friendships and being popular. I had to be the handsome cool guy with money. I drove my friends around in my father's Mercedes and paid for their dinners. I wanted people to perceive I could date any girl I wanted. I worked hard to be the guy everyone wanted to be. It only took a few weeks for all that, my life's work, to be gone entirely. I couldn't dance anymore; all of my dancing solos went to my most prominent rival, who eventually became my girlfriend's dancing partner. None of my Armenian friends wanted to visit me. I was a buzzkill. My non-Armenian friends weren't allowed to visit me because my parents forbade it. I had lost everything.

Though it was hard to reconcile how significantly my life had shifted, in some ways, I think being able to let go of all those expectations was a good thing. In retrospect, it was freeing. Now, instead of finishing school and building a life in Iran, the thing that I looked forward to the most was the possibility of walking again. If I could just walk again, I could go to America. In the back of my mind, I hadn't forgotten my father's promise.

The prospect of going to America was my sole source of optimism throughout my recovery. I was willing to try anything anyone suggested for a speedy recovery. If someone said to take one thousand milligrams of calcium a day, I would take it. If someone had a particular root for me to eat, I would eat it. I rubbed donkey oil on my feet. I know you may think I am joking, but it's believed in Armenian culture that the fat from a donkey has healing powers. It's expensive and scarce. Fortunately, my parents knew where to find it. If I wasn't rubbing it on my feet, I ate it in a capsule. I ate chicken feet stew and pig ear stew. If there was anything, no matter where it came from, that promised to give strength, I was willing to try it and try it again. I was determined to walk. The only trouble is that now, after trying so many things, I can't definitively say if it was the donkey oil or the chicken feet stew that ultimately did it. Oh well, I was healing.

Even though none of my non-Armenian friends were allowed to visit and most of my Armenian friends didn't want to visit, I did have two close Armenian friends, Saban and Artin, who were there for me during my recovery. They visited and made me feel like I was still a normal person. But it was a sharp decline in the number of friends I thought I had before the accident.

Plenty of my parent's friends stopped by to wish me well. Typically, during these visits, they visited me in the living room for a few minutes and then left to sit with my parents in the dining area a few feet away. My mom served coffee, tea, and snacks, and everyone sat at the dining table and chatted. Mind you, there were couches and places to sit near me, but the dining table was almost always the preferred seating choice. I think spending too much time around me made many of my visitors feel uncomfortable. Not sitting with me also gave them an opportunity to talk candidly about the accident, hypothesizing what might have really happened. Within earshot, I heard things like:

"Harma must have been speeding."

"If he had been driving a Mercedes instead of a Paykan, it wouldn't have happened."

"It had to have been the rain."

"Thank goodness it was Ashura Tasu'a and the roads were empty. It could have been much worse."

People even doubted the second accident had happened. Many people thought I had just hit the bus and made up the second accident to deflect blame. Only after my father hired a private investigator to look into who was at fault did he confirm that there had, indeed, been a third car and a driver who disappeared. The entire ordeal was enraging. Once, while a few guests were discussing my accident, I became so upset, I squeezed the water glass I was holding so hard that I crushed it in my hand and had to get stitches. Whenever I sat and listened to everyone's opinion about what had happened, I couldn't help but think, *I know what happened. I lost my friends. I lost my school. I lost my ability to walk. That's what happened!* Nobody was there but me; nobody was an expert on what had happened but me. Their opinions were bullshit, and they just added noise—sadly, the only noise in what had become a painfully silent existence.

All I heard the day before the accident was how amazing my legs were—some kind of irony. I can't help but wonder if things had been just a bit different, if I hadn't gone to the church to see the old woman or seen the vision of the man in my front seat, would I be dead? I'll never know, but I choose to believe there is a reason everything happened the way it did and that reason is who and where I am today.

◇◇◇

Feeling invisible while people sat around me and pontificated about how I caused my accident is an experience that highlights a valuable lesson. The people who talk the loudest and have the strongest opinions, especially unsolicited opinions, often have zero substance behind their beliefs. I don't listen to people who offer unsolicited opinions because often the only thing they are interested in hearing is their own voice.

14. The Military

Sometimes to serve in the military, you have to serve your sergeant.

NINE TERRIBLE BEDRIDDEN MONTHS PASSED. Finally, I was strong enough to use a wheelchair. But instead of getting on with some semblance of my life, I had to apply for my military service form. In Iran, every man must serve in the military at some point. If you are attending college, you can defer your service until after you graduate. Upon graduation, your newfound expertise and education typically warrant you a more senior position. Those who aren't enrolled in college must apply at eighteen. Being an American citizen didn't exempt me from serving, as Iran didn't recognize my dual citizenship. Being disabled also didn't exempt me from having to serve; it just meant I would have to serve differently.

Joining the military felt much like the start of yet another new chapter. Up to now, there had been so many changes in my life. I had switched schools often. I had been enrolled in college and then left after my accident. This simply seemed like another turn on my path. I also viewed it as an opportunity. Nobody knew me there. Nobody knew I was "feminine" or had any preconceived notions of how I should or shouldn't act. It was a fresh start. I was a blank canvas. I made a promise to myself to present as masculine as possible so no one would suspect there was anything different about me.

The first three months of service was all training. Not necessarily training for combat—I wasn't able to participate in that anyway. This was training on Iranian patriotism, and one of the training exercises that we did required marching. I didn't want to participate for obvious reasons. I was in a wheelchair, and it made zero sense to me why I should learn how to march—I was physically incapable of it.

Unfortunately, reason lost out to the rules, and my sergeant made it clear there were no exceptions. I would just have to follow behind the rest of the soldiers in my wheelchair as we learned the routines. Painted on the ground were two flags, the American flag and the Israeli flag. We were taught to march across both flags in a show of disrespect to what were considered Iranian enemies. Even though I was an American citizen, I participated because I didn't want to make waves, and I knew the faster I got training done, the quicker I could get on with my service and be done with it. But I also did not take any of it seriously. I asked to go to the bathroom during our marches, made funny movements, purposely moved outside of unison—what a waste of my time.

The first two weeks were very uncomfortable because I felt I couldn't trust anyone. I was perpetually worried about what they might think of me. I gravitated toward people who, in that group, struck me as minorities. I felt they might be less likely to presume things about me or judge me. In the end, it didn't take me long to gain the trust and respect of some people. Something I have always been good at.

My sergeant, who was a bit older than me, took to me quickly. He was rough around the edges but handsome. He was taller than I was, but I suppose most people are taller than me. He was thin but clearly in great shape, similar to a swimmer's build. He had light hazel eyes and short hair and wore a hat. After a while, I started to feel that familiar feeling. His gazes were a little too long, and his energy toward me seemed different than with the other guys. I could tell that he was like me.

Eventually, during training, I transitioned from wheelchair to walker. My sergeant told me I didn't have to march anymore and I could do work in the office he ran just outside the dormitories. Why it made sense to wait until I could actually march to put me on desk duty is beyond me. But whatever the thought behind it, I was happy about it. After all, the office was very quiet, and very few people came in and out other than him.

Due to the sheer numbers of men who had joined up and the lack of necessity for such a large reserve of soldiers, a law was passed that allowed soldiers to pay to have their mandatory service of two years cut down, which allowed them to get their "paper" sooner. Paper was a signed document confirming you had served the required amount of time. It was common for wealthier Iranians to pay for this. I was fortunate this law passed during my service and my family had the money to pay for it.

One day my sergeant cornered me and asked why I was buying my military service. I told him that I was born in the US, and I wanted to shorten my military service because I planned to leave Iran as soon as I finished. Probably not the best thing to share with an Iranian sergeant. The next day he ordered me to march across the American flag. Afterward, he pulled me aside and told me I would never get my paper as long as he was my sergeant. I was horrified. The only thing that had kept me going throughout this entire ordeal was the prospect of being able to leave Iran and go to the US. After everything I had been through, I was being told I couldn't go, but I wouldn't let a sergeant stand in my way. I just had to figure out a way around this.

My recovery was progressing really well. Though I was still using a walker, I was finally able to drive myself, and, surprisingly, my father was perfectly willing to let me drive his Mercedes to the base. I started to feel like myself again. I cared more about my appearance than I had since before the accident. I dressed better and styled my hair, and people took notice. Particularly my sergeant. I knew his interest in me would be the best way to get back on his good side. I started to buy things I knew he would like, and then I would pretend I had purchased them for myself and didn't want them anymore and ask if he wanted to take it off my hands. He always did. I did this with a bottle of cologne, a luxury item in Iran, especially for people who were not wealthy. Once, while wearing it, he whispered to me in Farsi, "It reminds me of you when I wear this." How ironic for a man to tell that to another man in a language spoken by one of the most homophobic cultures in the world.

Last day of serving in the military.

After my three-month training had ended, the sergeant told me he wanted me to extend my service with him, working in the office instead of going on to the next level. I agreed, thinking this would be the best way to stay in his favor and get my paper. My father was an opium smoker, and even though I had never tried it, I knew it was a very popular drug in Iran. I decided to raise the stakes from just casually giving gifts by asking the sergeant whether he smoked opium as well. He told me he did. I proposed going up to my parent's garden house to smoke opium. I told him we could go up and make kebabs and that there was vodka as well. I knew that because he was a Muslim, he couldn't outwardly express interest in drinking liquor, but I wanted to make sure he knew it was available to him in case it might sweeten the pot. Sure enough, he jumped on the invitation.

I drove us up in the Mercedes, and we did exactly what I had proposed. He smoked opium, we ate kebab, and he drank vodka. I remained sober.

After building a fire, he grabbed me and said, "You understand I don't want you to go to the US, don't you?"

"I don't understand. Why do you care?"

"Because I will be here. You can get married, and I can get married, but we both can be here together."

Knowing I had already fucked up once by telling him I planned to leave, I wasn't going to make that mistake again. I told him that once he gave me my paper, he could have me and I wouldn't want to leave after that anyway. But he would have to provide me with my paper if he wanted me. That pissed him off—not because he understood what I was trying to do but because he wanted me then. He became aggressive, threw me on the ground in front of the fireplace, pushed my head down, and forced himself on me. I didn't want it. What happened was not consensual, but I went along with it because I was scared of things escalating. We were completely alone, and I now knew this immensely dangerous secret about him. He liked men. If I resisted, I worried he might hurt me or worse.

When he finished, he asked, "Did you enjoy it?"

I told him, "I can't wait to continue this."

But that was a lie. He was the only one who enjoyed that. And it wasn't just the sex that he enjoyed. It was the power he was wielding over me. Then we went to bed. It was the longest night of my life. And that's coming from someone who laid in bed unable to walk for months.

A week passed, and we kept our distance. I think perhaps we were both fearful of the secret we now shared. As the second part of training was set to begin. I was called into his office. As I walked in, I was shaking with fear. I didn't know what to expect. Would he embarrass me? Had he told anyone? What had happened at the garden house was traumatizing, and I had no clue what was waiting for me when I got to his office. Without looking at me, he handed me my paper. It was signed. He told me I didn't have to stay or complete my service. I was done. He had assaulted me, and the one thing that tied me to him was gone. I was free. Despite the fact that this man had assaulted me, I felt sorry for him that he actually thought we could be together, leading double lives and reserving our passion for one another. My feelings about this experience and my sergeant are incredibly complicated, but I do still feel sorry for him. I do find myself wondering what his life is like today and whether he continues to live in a prison of his own sexuality. I worry that he has victimized other men and wonder whether he even realizes the trauma he inflicted.

I will never know exactly why he changed his mind, but if his intention was to get rid of me, he succeeded. I caught a cab and left. As I rode, I couldn't help but wonder whether any of the blame over what had happened should be placed with me. My head was swimming with questions. Was I a victim? Was I manipulative? Had I caused this? Had I wanted this? I got what I wanted. Was this an embarrassment or an achievement?

◇ ◇ ◇

It is so important to accept where you've been in life if you want to get where you are going. Life won't be a comfortable journey if you deny the things that have happened to you. I had a challenging childhood, was in a terrible accident, and was assaulted. That is the reality. Those events shaped who I am and color how I approach every situation, whether intentionally or unintentionally. Everyone has a story, and there are reasons for why people act the way they do. If someone struggles to connect, maybe they are afraid of being judged harshly because they were emotionally abused. On the flip side, if someone is an extrovert, perhaps they are looking for validation because they struggle with validating themselves. That isn't to say there is something negative attached to every personality trait or attribute any of us have. More so, it is to say our experiences shape who we are, how we interact with others, and how we approach life's challenges long after we make peace with those experiences.

15. Leaving Iran

When the plane left, we flew into a completely unknown situation, but I knew it would be better.

AFTER I GOT MY PAPER, I didn't waste any time. I was going to America. I immediately took two of my friends and went to the office where you get a separate paper necessary to apply for your passport. My friends had to lift me up the long stairs because I was still using a walker. As I passed the men walking in and out in their military outfits, I could not help but think of my sergeant and feel nauseated. I got the second paper, left, and went straight to the passport office to apply for my passport. I even gave them extra money to expedite it. Despite everything that had happened, I could not help but feel ecstatic. I was so close.

Two weeks later, I went back to the passport office and picked up my passport. I sped home, found my father and said, "I'm walking, and I have my passport. Can I go to the US now?" With little hesitation, he agreed. He told me that I could go in the summer. It was December, and the Armenian community was in the middle of Christmas and New Year's celebration. Knowing that this would be my last Christmas and my last New Year's in Iran made it the best holiday I had ever had.

Deep down, my mother knew if I ever got the opportunity to go to the US, I was never going to come back. I am certain if she had not met my father, she would never have returned either. In the first week of January, I went and bought my ticket. My father expected me to buy an open ticket so I could leave in the summer, as we had discussed, but I was ready to go immediately, so I bought a flight for late February. It was roundtrip, but I knew I was never going to take that return flight. I felt like I had gotten my life back, and I didn't want to waste another day of it in a place I wanted no part of. I came home and thought up a plan to make it seem as though I had mistakenly bought a ticket for February. I enlisted one of my friends to help. While sitting in the room with my dad, my friend asked to see my ticket to the US. I pulled it out, showed it to him, and was sure to reiterate the fact that it was an open ticket. After examining the ticket, my friend proclaimed, "This isn't an open ticket. It's for February twenty-second!" I pretended to be shocked and worried. I apologized to my father for the mistake that I had made but also reminded him that it was nonrefundable. I don't know if he bought it or didn't care one way or the other, but he agreed to let me leave in February. He gave me his blessing and $2,400 for the trip.

The final piece to the puzzle was getting an American passport. It had been taken from me as a baby when my father forced my mother to move back to Iran after having my sister. There was no American embassy in Iran. Instead, my mother and I went to the Swiss embassy, which assists Americans in Iran. Almost immediately, they instructed us to go to a different Swiss embassy, one housed in a significantly nondescript location. Once I got there, I was astonished—everyone there was American. No one was Swiss. After proving my identity and citizenship, they told me they would prepare an American passport for me. However, they cautioned me against taking it, as having an American passport in Iran was a considerable risk and I would be considered a spy and arrested if anyone found out. Instead, they promised to have it ready for me at the airport when I came for my flight.

On February 22nd, we arrived at the airport, and after discretely asking around, we found a man who handed an envelope to my parents with my American passport in it. I said my goodbyes to my family, hugging them and wiping my mother's tears. I was not sad. Instead, I felt a combination of excitement and fear of the unknown. I was going to America on faith; I had no concept of what was in store for me there. I did not know whether I would like it or whether I would get along with my family in the US. I knew nothing except for the fact that it was not Iran. It would be different. Different how? I was not sure. But it would be different.

I made my way through security and finally got to the gate. In Iran, there was a final check where they

February 22, 2001. Arrived at LAX.

looked at your passport and visa one last time before you were allowed to board the plane. The lines were separated by men and women. I got into the men's line. In the corner of my eye, I could see my plane, framed by the beautiful glass windows and marble floors of the airport. The attendant abruptly asked, "Where are you going? Where is your visa?" I told him I was going to the US by way of Moscow, my first stop. There were no direct flights from Iran to the US. I did not have a visa. He asked me whether I had a green card. I told him no, I had only a passport. Confused, he said, "Oh, interesting, you have a US passport? Let me see it." Keep in mind, there was no reason for him to ask to see my passport. I had an Iranian passport, and my US passport was Russia's issue, not his. But he still wanted to see it. I took them out and passed them underneath the glass. He examined them, clearly taking note of the fact they were both brand new. With disdain, he pushed them back to me underneath the glass with such force, they flew off the counter and onto the marble floor. He said, "Go to your country and never come back."

Finally, I boarded the Aeroflot plane. Sitting in the middle seat, I was still nervous. I paid no attention to all the people boarding or the flight instructions. I didn't hear the pilot make any announcements or the attendants tell us to put on our seatbelts. I just waited nervously. As we pushed from the gate, my heart was pounding. Then, with a rush of speed and accompanying adrenaline, we ascended into the air. I felt the wheels retract into the plane. And that was it. At that moment, I began to sob. I was done. I was finally done. They could not turn the plane around. They could not call me back to the airport. They could not call me back to Iran. It was over. I was free.

It had been just over a year since the accident that had made me lose everything and brought my entire life to a screeching halt. A year since I realized life was not guaranteed and I had to live it for myself and no one else. A year since I saw the vision of a man telling me I was going to die. Maybe I did die that day or at least some part of me. The dreams I had certainly did. The plans I had to live my life as my father had, join his business, marry a woman, be unfaithful and unhappy—those plans died. The person who thought that was enough died. In his place was someone who demanded to live.

◇ ◇ ◇

As my plane ascended into the air, I felt a rush of emotion. It felt like the hardest-fought victory in the history of the world. Despite everything that had happened, I had succeeded in escaping a life I knew I did not want to lead anymore. It was the setbacks that made it so sweet. No matter what the success is, whether personal, professional, or otherwise, remembering the obstacles that stood in your way makes the celebration so much sweeter.

16. LA at Last

Armenians go to Glendale. Persians go to Beverly Hills. Somehow, I ended up in West Hollywood. I wonder why?

I WAS WIRED FOR BOTH FLIGHTS, Iran to Moscow and Moscow to Los Angeles. I couldn't have slept if I'd tried. I did not know what lay ahead for me in LA, but I knew it would be more. It would be true. And it would not have been possible if I hadn't gotten into the accident.

As the wheels touched down at LAX, I felt a little bit like a fish staring out of its fishbowl at the strange world beyond the glass. I didn't speak any English, so the instructions from the pilot and flight attendant were gibberish to me, though I was too overcome with excitement to pay attention anyway. Once we made it to the gate, I jumped up to get off of the plane before everyone else. Many of the people flying with me were Russians, and I was an American citizen. I assumed in a place like the US, American citizens deplaned first. I had heard of America's patriotism, and even though this wasn't practiced on Iranian flights, it seemed like a great way to pay respect to American citizens (like myself). Unfortunately, given the number of non-American citizens who also jumped out of their seats, it seemed this was, in fact, not an American tradition but rather something I'd just dreamed up.

On the second leg of my flight, I sat next to a Persian man who also spoke Farsi. He helped me off the plane and asked whether I was a citizen. He helped direct me to the customs line, and I, using my crutches, very *very* slowly made my way there. Once I got to customs, the customs agent asked for my passport and how long I had been out of the country. Unfortunately, I couldn't understand a word (so obviously, quite some time). The customs agent was also confused by the fact that my passport did not have a stamp. Typically, when you travel from the US and come back, you have some sort of stamp in your passport from wherever you went. Mine was brand spankin' new. As if all that wasn't enough to make me look out of place, I was covered in bright yellow gold jewelry. Knowing deep down I was never coming back to Iran, my mom gave me jewelry as a bit of a makeshift savings account. If I got low on cash, I could sell it. But I didn't want to have to declare any of it in customs. So, naturally, I just wore it all. Worried the customs agent might think there was some sort of foul play, I found the Persian man I had befriended on the plane and had him translate for me. He explained my unique situation, how I was an American citizen but had lived my entire life in Iran. I'm not sure I would have been let through so quickly if it weren't for him. Afterward, I found baggage claim and grabbed my bags. Again, still recovering from my accident, I found a way to ask people for their help lifting my luggage and getting every-thing to the sliding doors. And then, finally, I saw a familiar face.

My grandmother, Uncle A, my mom's brother, and my aunt were waiting for me just beyond the baggage claim. We said our hellos and jumped in the car. I would love to say how amazing it was to finally be in LA and drive through the city while absorbing the sites. But, as Armenian culture seems to dictate, our first and only stop was Glendale. Armenian mecca. It seems no matter where Armenians go in life, they always come back to Glendale. Personally, if I had my way, I'd prefer we be like the Persian Jews who congre-gate in Beverly Hills. But that's just me.

I moved in with my grandmother and my Uncle A and had been in Glendale all of three days before I called my parents and told them

I was not coming back to Iran. It wasn't a blunt announcement. I softened the landing by telling them I wanted to resume my studies in LA and enroll in the community college. My father was livid and would not entertain the idea whatsoever. He made it clear that if I didn't come back, he would no longer support me financially. I would also be disinherited and never receive any of his business after he died. I was OK with that.

Since I had been cut off by my dad, I needed to find work quickly. Fortunately, my cool uncle had a messenger service, and taking up work with him was an excellent way for me to learn the streets of LA. He even got me a Nextel phone, which was somewhere between a beeper and a real cell phone. And of course, a messenger's bible—a Thomas Guide, or as I think of it, Google Maps before Google Maps.

I also want to mention my aunt and her husband. They are two of the most generous people I have ever known. I wasn't in LA for long before I realized having a car would be a necessity. One day I found my way to a used car dealership on San Fernando Road. After perusing a bit, I saw the coolest car that I had ever seen. It was a red Nissan SX, a sexy coupe with the headlights that look like winking eyelids that open and shut. If I could have that car, I would never want another car again for the rest of my life. The dealer wanted $4,300 for it, but I had only $1,500. I jumped on my Nextel and called my aunt's husband. He came down to the dealership and paid the other $2,800. The car was mine.

At that time, Uncle A was engaged to a beautiful woman. Though I had never met her until I moved to America, she felt like close family—as if we had known each other for years. She was kind, warm, and bright. One night, my Uncle A, his fiancée, and I stopped at the gas station. Uncle A got out of the car to pump gas. A few moments later, his fiancée gasped and pointed to the distance as if she were showing me a rare animal.

"Look! Do you know who that is?" she said.

"No clue. Who is it?" I replied.

She was pointing toward a fancy Mercedes, so I knew the person must be rich. But I still was not sure who it was. Filled with excitement, she explained it was a very famous Armenian hairdresser who did hair for Armenian celebrities and the most elite Armenian women. I had never heard of him, and to be honest, I wasn't that interested. Until she told me he liked men; she said he was gay. That caught my attention. I had heard the term *gay* a few times but did not have a clear idea what it meant. I filed away what she said for later. When I got home, I found my grandmother's Yellow Pages and looked up the hairdresser. Once I saw his phone number, I drove to a payphone and called him at his salon. He picked up!

In Armenian, I said, "I'm new to this country. I'm not gay, but I *have* been with men. Where can I go and find more men?"

"I'll take you there. Who are you?"

"Nice try. You are never going to know who I am. But I am going to test you to see if you ever tell anybody."

After that, I became obsessed with him. I wasn't interested in him romantically, but I was obsessed with the idea of him being an out gay man. Especially a gay Armenian. After that, we started talking on the phone regularly, but we never agreed to meet. After going back and forth several times, he finally asked me what I was afraid of. I told him I didn't want him to tell everyone that I was like him. Because I wasn't. He decided to meet me in the middle. He told me to meet him out off of San Fernando Road, and we would go to the Abbey in West Hollywood, the gayest neighborhood in Los Angeles.

◇◇◇

I have immense respect for the hairdresser. Being out and proud, nearly twenty years ago, was no small feat. Coming from our culture and as a public figure, it was shockingly brave. I couldn't understand why he would come out when he could have a simple life. I understand it now. Now that I am out and have a family and a community that knows me for who I am, it makes perfect sense. He had accepted himself and wanted to live in truth and refused to let his sexuality or his culture get in the way of his success. I may not have realized it then, but he was very much an inspiration.

17. The Abbey

*If only switching between gay and straight was an Olympic sport, I
would have brought home the gold.*

HE PICKED ME UP in his white Mercedes. A typical choice—it's an
Armenian thing. You may have never noticed, but we Armenians
drive only white or black cars. It must be a rule somewhere. The fancy
car did little to calm my nerves. I was a big ball of fear. He was surprised by how young I was. I think it made him even more protective
over me. In Armenian, he told me not to be nervous. But I couldn't
help it. I was nervous about where we were going. I wanted him to
protect me, but I also was afraid of him. I had so many ideas about
what could potentially happen. I did not want to be taken advantage
of again. I remained tense the entire car ride; my hands clasped tightly
in my lap, I kept my focus on the city beyond my passenger window.
I thought even the slightest movement in his direction might invite
conversation, which I was not prepared for. We rode in silence.

After what seemed like two hours, but was probably only about
thirty minutes, we arrived in West Hollywood. He parked his car,
and we walked over to the Abbey. If you have ever been to West
Hollywood and visited the Abbey, you are probably thinking of an
impressive Mediterranean structure with an expansive patio, outdoor
seating, polished concrete floors, and polished patrons. That's the Abbey
now, arguably the most popular gay club in Los Angeles and among

the most prominent in the country. Back then, the Abbey was much different than it is now. It was much smaller. It had a fun, relaxed vibe. I don't think I was even carded. This was before gay bars were trendy and attracted everyone from actual gay men to their best girlfriends, bachelorette parties, and straight guys looking for another drink in the midst of barhopping. Back then, the Abbey was first and foremost a refuge for gay men where they could be themselves unapologetically. It was the perfect place to take a confused closet case like me. Nonetheless, at that time, my social life consisted of the Glendale gas station and my grandmother's house, and the Abbey was downright scary. I begged him, for the love of God, do not introduce me to anyone. I could not muster the nerve to be social. My pleading fell on deaf ears. He proudly showed me off to all of the regulars he knew and acknowledged each with a brief head nod as we walked by. I didn't drink any alcohol, though it probably would have helped. I wanted to keep my wits about me. I sipped my cup of water frequently as a way to occupy myself, keeping my cup close to avoid any potential drugging situation. More importantly, if someone took a sip of it, who knew what I could catch? (Fucked up, I know.)

I took it all in, and there was A LOT to take in. I stared at everyone, devoting just a bit of time to each man. I was like Arnold Schwarzenegger's Terminator except I wasn't scanning each person to determine whether they were a target; I was just trying to figure out whether they liked men. My head was spinning as I thought, *Does this one like guys? That one can't like guys.* It was all so foreign to me. There were so many kinds of men. An Asian man passed, and I thought, *Wow, there are Asian people here too!* A buff man walked by. *Is that what a hot body is?* I had never grown up with men who looked like this. It was difficult for me to understand what exactly the American standards of male attractiveness were—harder still, gay American standards of male attractiveness. A guy came up to me and put his hand on my face. He looked into my eyes and with a smile he said, "You are gorgeous!"

I took his hand and swatted it away in disgust then grabbed his face the same way he had grabbed mine and said, "FUCK YOU! YOU'RE GORGEOUS!" I turned to my escort and asked him in Armenian what the insult meant that was just hurled at me. He told me it meant I was attractive. Oops! Embarrassed, I begged him to explain to the guy that I didn't speak English.

After we left, the hairdresser drove me back to my car, and I thanked him for taking me. I got in my Nissan and sped home, still reeling from the night. I could barely sleep. The next day I called him and asked if he would go with me again. Surprisingly, he agreed. The second evening was much like the first. I barely said anything, just stared at everyone, still stunned this was real life. And, like the previous night, I got dropped off at my car and went home. The next day I called him again and asked if he'd take me. This time he said no. Well, his loss. I didn't need him to go to the Abbey. But I did need his directions. I whipped out my Thomas Guide and navigated to his salon. Afterward, I went to his salon unannounced and asked him whether he would show me how to get there. Maybe he wanted to get rid of me, or perhaps he was impressed by my resolve, but he showed me the route. From then on, I went to the Abbey every single night. It was the only bar I felt comfortable in.

My family had no idea where I went at night and fortunately didn't ask. At my college, I met a beautiful Armenian girl, and we started dating. But our relationship required me to be a master at living a double life. A typical evening consisted of dinner or a movie together. Afterward, we would make out in my car. While we made out, I'd have one eye open, looking at my watch behind her head to see what time it was. We couldn't waste too much time; otherwise, I wouldn't be able to get to the Abbey and make it home early enough not to raise any questions. Every night I kept a change of clothes in my trunk like a high school girl who didn't want her parents to know about the skimpy clothes she wore for school. I wanted to wear skimpy outfits too! I wore skintight T-shirts that hugged my biceps and stopped just at my waist, so when I raised my arms, you would be able to see my stomach. Honestly, if transforming into a homo was an Olympic sport, I would have taken home the gold. Every night, right before I got home, I changed back into my boring "straight" clothes.

When I was at the Abbey, I never drank. Not a single drop of alcohol. Just water. I also never stayed out too late or went home with anyone. I was simply an observer. For me, going to the Abbey was about nothing more than being present in this world that I had never known existed. It was my safe space where I was able just to be. I can't say I was able to be myself there. I didn't know who I was yet. And perhaps in many ways, I was simultaneously inching toward the real me. It wasn't about partying or sex. It was about feeling a connection with people like me. I felt it through the music and the lights. The genuine happiness people had to be among each other. I lived vicariously through them. I connected with them, even if that connection was simply about sharing energy more than making friends.

I had been living the double life for weeks without so much as a peep from my girlfriend or my family. That all changed one night when I got home and noticed the light in the basement was still on. It was after midnight, and everyone was typically in bed by this hour. No sooner did I tiptoe into the house than my Uncle A cornered me.

"Where do you go at night?" he asked.

I didn't answer. My palms were drenched in sweat.

"Where do you go at night?" This time, he yelled.

"Why do you want to know?" I tried my best to keep cool.

"A friend of mine saw you going to a bad place . . ."

Even now, thinking back to this exchange, I can't help but think of it as a standoff. Like something out of a Western. We both knew the truth; we both knew where I had been. I suppose we were waiting to see who would crack first. We continued.

"That's interesting that a friend of yours saw me in a bad place. What were they doing there?" I asked with the slightest hint of defiance in my tone.

"He was looking for a job," Uncle A responded quickly.

"So was I. I was looking for a job too."

Finally breaking with the ridiculous pretense of our conversation, Uncle A said, "You know, there are programs out there that can help fix you, right?"

"When you grow up with something, a difference that is so obvious, so clear to so many people, a difference that is repeated by every school kid on the playground, every teacher, every principal, you get to a point where you no longer believe you are fixable."

I was right. I didn't realize it then, but I *was* right. I wasn't confident in the fact I was gay. I still wasn't able to truly identify as being gay. But I knew I was different, and I knew it wasn't something anyone would be able to fix. I had always been this way. In a perfect world, if an uncle found out that his nephew was gay, he would reaffirm their mutual love and support and welcome this truth with open arms. But the world isn't necessarily that perfect. At least my world wasn't. He was kind, which was his nature. Uncle A was an immensely kind and loving man. As such, he approached the issue with compassion, albeit misguided compassion. He wanted to find solutions to what he perceived as a grave problem. The only trouble was, I was starting to no longer see it as one.

We continued discussing the same points, merely talking in circles. Uncle A eventually realized that I wasn't going to back down, and his compassion started to wane. Sternly, he told me that if I was going to stay in his home, then I had to be home by 10:00 p.m. In his mind, this was the best way to keep me from going out and continuing to be exposed and corrupted by gay culture. Good luck.

The next morning when I woke up, still bleary-eyed, I overheard my name from downstairs. It was my aunt's voice, but she wasn't calling for me. She was on the phone, talking about me. I knew the only person she would be talking to would be my mother. I quietly picked up the extension upstairs and started to listen in. I was only partly right. It wasn't just my aunt and my mother. Both of my aunts, my grandmother, and my mother were all on some sort of Armenian conference call. The topic at hand: How do you solve a problem like Harma? With a great deal of worry in her voice, my aunt said to my mother, "*You have* to come to the US as soon as possible. Harma is only going out with men, and he is going to get AIDS." After that, I tuned out and didn't hear much of what was discussed. I knew my days living with my family were numbered. I knew it was becoming an unsustainable living situation. Even then, even as I was starting to see this secret slowly coming to light, I still felt confused by the interest everyone had. After all, I was still dating a woman. I felt that from my family's vantage point, I was doing exactly what I was supposed to do. What difference did it make if, on my own time, in private, I indulged in something that was of no consequence to anyone? Wasn't that the Armenian way? In hindsight, I realize I was confused by the fact that it was becoming more obvious I wouldn't be able to lead a double life in the US the way so many people did in Iran.

◇ ◇ ◇

It is incredibly frightening to go against your culture and community. Humans gravitate toward one another, and we often find comfort in the shared identities and experiences within communities we create versus those we are born into. Growing up Armenian in Iran, our culture was extremely important because we had to fight to hold onto it. Honor, shame, standards, and reputation are all aspects of my culture that I learned to understand and respect at a young age. But my culture did not support who I was becoming. So I had to make a decision. Either choose my community or me. I chose myself. Even if the environment you are a part of doesn't support who you feel you are in your heart, you still have to follow it. Family will express love and concern because they want what's best for you. That doesn't mean they are right.

18. Finding My Independence

Did I want to clean bathrooms?
Absolutely not. Did I need a job? Yes.

WHEN I FIRST MOVED to the US, my aunt recommended I get on food stamps. It wasn't uncommon for Armenians to go on food stamps and assistance when they first moved to America to help with the transition. It made sense to me. Plus, I figured she knew better than I did what it took to get settled and make it in America. So, I did it. I signed up for $200 a month in food stamps. It was a valuable supplement to the money I was making as a messenger for Uncle A. And, after our disagreement, I hoped to soon find a new job so I no longer had to rely on my disapproving uncle for my livelihood.

A short while later, I met an Armenian man at the carwash. I can't remember his name, but to be honest, I sometimes think of him as an angel. He certainly, in a brief yet impactful way, altered the course of my life. We struck up a conversation, and I told him that I had just moved to the US, and I was on food stamps. His response was one of the most powerful things anyone has ever said to me. "The sooner you get off of government help, the sooner you can start helping the government." It took me a while to fully understand what he meant. He meant I was better off being as self-reliant as possible. In a country like the US, I would find fulfillment in paving my own way. Kindly, he gave me the name and address of a man he thought might be hiring help.

The next day, at the crack of dawn, I pulled out my Thomas Guide and looked up the address the man had given me and mapped my route. I needed to find work and become independent from my family.

I arrived at a vast warehouse space in an industrial area of the city. Ramps were leading to garage doors that had to have been three stories high. There were trucks everywhere. Not eighteen-wheelers but the mid-sized trucks you see that often carry things like appliances or furniture. Dozens of men were walking around, loading and unloading the trucks, each with the facial expression of someone with a purpose. Perhaps it was the time I had spent working for my father at his warehouse, but with just a quick scan of the area, I was able to zero in on who I thought was most likely in charge. I walked over to introduce myself.

He was the foreman. In Armenian, I explained I had been told I could find a job there. Cutting me off before I had even finished, he dismissed me and told me that he didn't know who I had spoken with, but there was no job to be had there. He walked away. I easily could have jumped in my car and headed home to Glendale, but that wasn't my style. I stuck around and waited for all the trucks to be loaded and be on their way.

By 9:00 a.m., the trucks had cleared, and things had finally started to slow down. I walked up one of the ramps and into the warehouse through a huge garage door. It was then that I was able to get a better idea of what exactly they did there. There were rolls, massive rolls. I got closer to one and realized they were rolls of carpet. This was a carpet distributor. I later found out they supplied and installed carpet for big-box stores like Home Depot and Lowe's. Every day, they'd get a list of addresses, load up the trucks with carpet rolls, go to the addresses, and install the carpets.

I had no permission to be there, but I walked through the warehouse as if I did. I noticed there were small, dirty pieces of carpet that looked like scraps from larger rolls. It was obvious they were meant to be discarded, but no one had gotten to it yet. I also saw a dumpster. Well, naturally, I picked up the scraps and took them to the dumpster. I walked back into the warehouse to collect more scraps, and just then, the foreman appeared out of nowhere. Confused, he walked over to me and asked me what I thought I was doing. I pleaded with him again, explaining that I really *really* needed a job. I would do anything. I would pick up trash. I would clean restrooms. I just needed to work.

I don't know if it was the desperation, the initiative, or a combination of them both, but it seemed to do the trick. He walked me toward the back of the warehouse into a small office, and we had a brief conversation that ended in him offering me $650 every two weeks. I was to be there every morning at 7:00 a.m., and I could leave at 4:30 p.m. I didn't know what I would be doing or whether $650 every two weeks was a reasonable amount of money to earn for it . . . but it was a job! I didn't think; I just said yes.

I left the warehouse and immediately went to call my parents and tell them I was going to move out of my family's home and get my own place. I asked whether they would be willing to give me an extra $500 a month to ensure I had enough money to cover my expenses. Surprisingly, they agreed.

A few days before I moved out, I came home from work and found my grandmother doing my laundry. She found a small T-shirt, one I had reserved for my nights in West Hollywood. She was crying.

She said, "Oh my God, I messed this up! I shouldn't have put this T-shirt in the dryer. It shrank!"

I looked at her and said, "No, this is how it's supposed to be."

Then I took the shirt from her so I could put it away. I couldn't help but think how completely foreign my nights at the Abbey might seem to her, how all of the men lived lives and were part of a community she legitimately could never even fathom. I suppose it was only recently that I could fathom it myself.

I found a studio apartment I could afford in a pretty rundown area of Glendale. Most of the people who lived there were poor and had recently moved to the US. It was a far cry from my family's home in the better part of Glendale and certainly a far cry from what I had become used to in Iran. Nonetheless, I was elated. I was equal parts happy and shocked. I could not believe, after all this time, I finally had my own place and could come and go as I pleased! Every night when I came home, I lit a candle. Not because lighting a candle was of any particular significance to me. But the ritual, just the simple act of doing something for myself in my own space, made me feel like my life was changing and I was in control.

After I moved into my own place, my life started to open up. I had a job. I was slowly learning English. I was making my own money. I was even beginning to build a social life. I felt comfortable talking to people when I went out at night, and eventually, I started making friends. One night when I was at the Abbey, I recognized an extremely well-known Persian entertainer. In fact, I used to dance to his songs. My grandmother often made fun of him whenever he was on TV because he was extremely flamboyant. I must have been staring at him, because we caught one another's eyes—likely because he could tell I was Middle Eastern and knew who he was. He walked over to me and, in Farsi, said, "Do you speak Farsi?" I responded in English, "No, I don't." I was an idiot.

As quickly as I realized the mistake I had made, the paranoia started to creep in. I began to feel, as irrational as it may have been, that this Persian entertainer was going to out me to the entire Armenian community. We came from similar cultures; he knew how taboo it was. He struck me as a gossip. Of course, this would be how everyone found out. How could I have been so dumb and reckless? This was what I got for coming here so often. This was bound to happen.

He laughed off my gaffe and told me to come with him. Still a bit uneasy and unsure of the situation, I followed him. He had a table and bottle service and was sitting with two other Armenians. They were incredibly friendly and asked me my name. I had two choices: I could either get the hell out of there, or I could give them the wrong name in the hopes that if and when they told other Armenians about me, nobody would know who it had been. The idea that we were all gay and all Middle Eastern—and thus all exposed to the same type of ridicule I was so immensely afraid of—never crossed my mind. I gave them a fake name.

Comfortable with my fake identity, I relaxed a little bit but not much. Likely sensing my unease, one of the Armenians asked me if I had ever been to GALAS. I had no clue what he was talking about. It was an acronym, and it stood for the Gay and Lesbian Armenian Society. I scoffed to myself. After all, it was hard enough for me to even sit with other gay Armenians. How could I join a society of them? Even so, I filed it away in the back of my head and looked it up later. The idea of hanging out with other gay Armenians didn't necessarily appeal to me, but one aspect of it did; when I looked them up, the information I found said they helped Armenian parents and relatives accept their gay family members. I thought I might just need that help at some point, so I started going to their center regularly. It was one of the best decisions I have ever made.

Going to GALAS made me feel like I wasn't a pariah, despite how I had felt for so long. I started making friends and building a network. They hosted events and dances, and they were some of the best nights I ever had in my life. I danced like I used to dance back in Iran. I didn't care how masculine or feminine I looked, and neither did anyone else. I was comfortable, a feeling I'm not sure I had ever really felt before.

GALAS often planned events and outings for us, and once they planned a camping trip. I was still working at the carpet company at this point, and I had struck up a friendship with my boss's sister, who also worked there. She was a tough cookie, no-nonsense kind of woman. There was little that was fun about her, and to be honest, she scared me. But I could tell she cared for me. By then, I had transitioned from picking up trash to scheduling appointments. It was a great way to learn English, and she monitored my phone conversations and corrected me when I said something wrong.

I needed a Friday off to be able to attend the camping trip. I went to her and asked whether I could have the day off, and she quickly agreed. I told her I was going on a camping trip, and she asked with whom.

Vaguely, I said, "Oh, it's a new group." I thought, *Am I about to come out? Should I come out? If I am going to, perhaps she is the best person to do it with. Maybe this can be like practice.*

She persisted with questions. "What group are you a part of? Where are you going camping?" she asked.

"It's a new group I just joined. We are going camping in a cemetery."

"A cemetery! Are you *sure* you want to belong to this group?" she asked, her voice equal parts confused and concerned.

I could sense her disapproval, and I started to become angry. How dare she criticize something she knew nothing about? "It's not a bad group! It's a good group. People just don't like them," I said in a huff, careful with my tone to not seem insubordinate.

"Groups who go to cemeteries are not normal," she shot back.

"What is so good about being normal?" I said.

"Fine, just be very careful when you are with them. I've never heard of this group, and it seems very odd. I just don't think a cemetery is a good place to go visit and camp for two nights."

I didn't care what she had to say. I was going on this camping trip. In a huff, I left and went to call one of my friends from GALAS. I told him my manager freaked out when I told her we were going to the cemetery.

"Why on earth would you tell her we are going to a cemetery?" My friend seemed as confused as my boss.

"Are we not going to the cemetery?"

"No, you idiot!" he replied. "We are going to Yosemite . . ."

Oops. I walked back upstairs and found the boss's sister. She was on a call, so I waited until she finished and pulled her aside.

"Do you remember when I told you I was going camping at a cemetery?" I asked.

"Yes . . ." She was still confused by the situation.

"We aren't going to a cemetery. We are going to Yosemite."

She erupted in laughter, dropping her phone. She could hardly breathe, and tears were welling in her eyes. I had never seen her laugh like that. To this day, she will text me now and then and ask me if I have any trips planned to the cemetery. I guess I still had some more English to learn.

Finding independence can be incredibly challenging. One of the things I love about my culture is there is a strong sense of family. People help each other. Families look out for each other. Parents don't just toss their kids out into the world and hope for the best, but they make an effort to help their children get on their feet. The downside of that is often it can feel smothering. When you are financially dependent on family, like it or not, they get a say or will try to have a say in what you do. For me, finding independence was not glamorous. I had to stay determined and work hard every single day. But it was essential for me to do so if I ever hoped to forge my own identity apart from my Armenian family.

19. Coming Out in America

A mother always knows. A girlfriend ... not so much.

UNCLE A'S WEDDING came not too long after I moved into my own place. In Armenian culture, weddings are a huge deal. Because so many families are spread out all over the world, weddings often serve as an opportunity for families to reunite. My mother and I stayed in contact regularly, and one day when we were talking about the wedding, I asked whether she thought Dad might let her come. Surprisingly, he said yes. Wanting to milk his goodwill for all it was worth, I asked whether my sister could come as well. Surprisingly, yet again, he said yes. Not only were they going to come to the wedding but they were going to stay for a few weeks to visit. Or at least, they were planning to stay for a few weeks to just visit.

When my mother and my sister arrived, they decided to stay with me in my studio apartment instead of staying with another family. Fitting the three of us required some creativity. I relocated my tiny dining table to the bathroom and put an extra mattress in its place. Whenever we had to shower, we moved the table out of the bathroom until we'd finished, and then back it went. Our furniture arrangement was fluid. The wedding came and went, but my mother and sister stayed with me in my apartment. I think they stayed because they missed spending time with me and because they enjoyed being in America. There were no other weddings on the horizon, so who knew when they might get another opportunity like this? Despite our extremely close quarters, it was a really happy time. We reconnected. It reminded me of the times when my father traveled on business and we would have the time of our lives simply enjoying each other's company.

But eventually, all things come to an end. After two months, my mother decided she needed to get back to Iran. My younger brother was still there; my father was his sole caretaker, and as we know, being nurturing was not exactly his strength. Though my mom had to get back, my parents agreed to let my sister stay behind after some convincing on my part. And poof, just like that, I became the guardian of a sixteen-year-old girl—a role I was happy to accept. I helped her enroll in a local high school and made sure she was taken care of. The question of whether it was a permanent arrangement never really came up, but as time progressed, it seemed more and more evident that it would be.

Though my sister staying in the US with me seemed to be a permanent situation, I knew my mother staying in Iran with my brother and father could not be. I had to figure out a way to get my mother and brother back to the US for good. Things were progressing that way. My father was becoming less domineering and closed off when it came to us spending time in America.

The trouble with bringing my brother to the US was that, unlike my sister and me, he was not an American citizen. At some point, he applied for and was given a green card, but it required my parents to travel to Italy to actually pick it up. They didn't, and the case eventually lapsed and was closed. I had to figure out a way to get that green card, and I needed to get creative to do it. With my mother in Iran, I decided I would write a letter on her behalf to the ambassador of the United States in Italy. In her voice, I explained she had two children who were both American citizens and living in the US, but her third child was not a citizen, and he was stuck in Iran. I told the ambassador my brother had been awarded a green card but never picked it up in Italy and essentially pleaded for them to reopen the case. I even told them her father was sick and it was becoming increasingly difficult to parent with her children living in separate countries. I gave them both my address in LA and my parents' address in Iran. I hoped, if we heard anything back, they would send it to both addresses, and I could ensure I was kept in the loop.

Miraculously, a few weeks later, I got a DHL package. It was a letter addressed to my mother and father. It said my brother could pick up his green card in Naples, but he had a limited amount of time to do it or the case would be closed for good. My father was completely in the dark about why a random DHL letter had shown up regarding my brother's green card, but he agreed to go to Italy and pick it up. While he did that, my mother traveled back to America.

After picking up my brother's green card, my father and my brother both traveled together to LA. Things had become less stringent, and my father no longer faced the same challenges in getting to the US that he had once experienced when we were babies. I still wonder why my father was so willing to allow everyone to come to the US for such an extended amount of time. I knew, deep down, we would never go back. I think he believed the opposite was true. I think he thought we would all visit, get it out of our systems, and come back to Iran. I think he felt there was nothing permanent in America for us. Our money, our property, his business, and his influence were all in Iran. All that was in America was some family and a different way of life.

Letting us go to America was also a way of controlling us. My father knew we enjoyed being in the US even if it was temporary. What better thing to hold over our heads to get what he wanted than to threaten us with forcing us to return if we ever did anything he didn't like. For example, when he arrived in LA, we all went to my grandmother's house for some family time. My father took this opportunity to demand an apology from my grandmother for being disrespectful when she and her now-dead husband had visited when I was a teenager. If she didn't apologize, he would force our entire family to leave and go back to Iran. I didn't dare to go to my father and tell him he couldn't make us do anything and we wouldn't go back to Iran regardless of what he did. Instead, I went to my grandmother and begged her to do as he wished. There was some utility in doing this. Despite my independence, I still needed my father's help to make ends meet. In the end, he was a true businessman and knew how to manipulate others to get what he wanted. He was effective.

Eventually, my father left us and traveled back to Iran. Just as he had with my sister, he agreed to let my brother stay in the US. I am sure he liked the idea of living a bachelor life without a kid holding him back. Now, we were finally together—all of us. With an ocean between the man who had tormented us and made our lives so challenging for so long and us, we could finally breathe. Before he left, he reiterated this was a temporary situation, and if I decided I never wanted to come back, he would stop paying for me. I took that as a call to action. I got a raise at my job, secured financial aid for my school, and prepared for what seemed like the inevitable. Once he left and I had my family with me, I knew I would never ever go back. And neither would they.

With our new living situation, I knew my studio wasn't sustainable for the four of us, so we started looking for a bigger place. We found a two-bedroom outside of Glendale in a less expensive area called Tujunga. It was more remote than Glendale, and we had only one car, which I needed to go to work and school. My family was essentially stranded during those times unless they could find other modes of transportation.

Despite the massive transition in my living situation and the general upheaval in my life, I still found time to maintain my social life. I still had a girlfriend, and I still was sneaking out to visit with my friends at GALAS and going out at night to West Hollywood.

Every time I left the house, my mother interrogated me. "Where are you going? Who are you going to be with? How long will you be gone?" Though time had passed, she hadn't forgotten what my aunt told her about my social life.

Eventually, by the time I was twenty-one, I felt like I couldn't hold on to the secret any longer and longed to tell someone how I had been feeling. I decided my sister was the safest person; she was seventeen. I trusted her, I didn't think she would judge me too harshly, and she would be an excellent test for potentially coming out to the rest of my family.

I took her out to lunch, and, as we sat, I just spilled my guts. I was gay. The first thing she said was, "Oh my God, Dad will kill Mom!" She wasn't speaking in hyperbole either. Her gut reaction was if my father found out I was gay, he would blame my mother and murder her for turning me that way. There was no thought of me, despite it being my truth. The secret, the act of being gay, was such a taboo in our culture. It was much bigger than me.

I think part of my desire to come out to someone was because things were starting to get serious with my girlfriend. She asked me to meet her parents. In Armenian culture, meeting a serious girlfriend's parents is essentially a pre-proposal. I knew that I could not marry her—or any woman, for that matter—and I had to pump the brakes on our relationship somehow and also confirm to myself that this, marrying her, would never happen. Coming out to my sister was one of my tactics. Simultaneously, I started to pull away from my girlfriend. I gave our relationship a curfew. We could no longer be out past 10:00 p.m. This was convenient because I knew that would give me enough time to go out afterward. But it also was effective in keeping her at arm's length.

One night, my girlfriend and I went out to the movies together. It was like any other date night. Except, to my mortification, a gay couple was sitting in the row in front of us. They were somewhat affectionate but not overly so. They engaged in the typical public displays of affection you would expect of a couple at a movie theater. Arm around the shoulders. Hand-holding. G-rated stuff. My girlfriend was disgusted by the sight and made sure to let me know. She said it was unnatural for two men to be together the way a man and a woman would be. I took her home, wondering if she were so adamant simply because she really had been that disgusted or because she wanted to send a clear message to me about how she felt about gay men in case I just happened to be one. In any event, her disgust didn't deter me from my regular post-date activities. Off to West Hollywood I went.

Later that night, when I came home, I found my mother and girl-friend sitting in the dark in our living room. I could tell just by looking at them that they both wanted to know exactly where I had been that night. It was also clear to me that they wanted to know for different reasons. My girlfriend wanted to see if I had been out sleeping with another woman, and I could sense the anger coursing through her just thinking about the prospect. My mother seemed to have a more hope-ful albeit wary disposition. She was *hoping* I had been out sleeping with another woman. My mother didn't miss a beat and immediately asked me where I had been. I told her I had been with another girl. Quickly, my girlfriend burst into tears, and my mother went to her, trying her best to console her. She hugged her, wiped her tears, and told her every-thing would be OK. Deep down, I am sure my mother felt a sense of relief, but she hid it well. My girlfriend collected herself and went home.

The next morning when I woke up, my mother was waiting for me. The conversation was not over. She asked if I had anything that I wanted to tell her. I don't know what about the previous night made me feel like it was time to come clean finally. Perhaps it was because the lie had become even more complicated. Maybe it was seeing my girlfriend in tears for no reason and realizing my actions were hurt-ing people I cared about. Perhaps all of the above? I told her there was something I wanted to say to her and asked if we could talk when I got home from work. She agreed, and as soon as I returned home, we went for a short drive around the neighborhood. I parked the car on a random street and prepared to tell her my biggest secret.

"Mom, I think you know what I am going to say," I said, looking straight out beyond the windshield, unable to make eye contact with her.

"No, I don't," she replied matter-of-factly.

"Not at all?"

"No."

I knew she was lying. I knew that after all of this time and the conversations she had had with my family, she knew deep down what was coming. One thing I had learned from GALAS is a mother almost always knows. In this instance, I felt even more strongly that my mother must know. We were so close and so in tune with one another. We were in many ways like siblings, not mother and son.

"I don't think I like women." The words fell out of my mouth so quickly and with such ease, it was hard to believe my entire life had just changed.

"It's OK. You are young, and sometimes you just don't want to see any woman," she responded assuredly.

"No, that isn't what I am saying. I am saying I don't think I like to be with a woman at all."

"You know, you've moved from one country to another, you had a huge accident, you are traumatized. Maybe this isn't the time to be thinking about a woman."

"Do you remember when I was twelve and you caught me playing with my friend?"

"I do, but every twelve-year-old boy plays with another boy."

"Well, do you remember when I was fifteen and you caught us underneath the stairs at our house?"

"You were fifteen. Fifteen-year-old boys do anything."

"Mom, you have seen me with men. OK, imagine a woman naked in front of you. Would you be able to go down on her?"

"Who?"

"You!"

"Absolutely not! That is disgusting!"

"Mom, I swear to God, that is exactly how I feel."

She demanded I drive her home immediately. I did as she wished. We rode in silence.

I decided I couldn't go back to our apartment. I didn't know where I was going to go, but I knew I needed space from my family. I drove away aimlessly, reeling from the conversation we had just had. My cell phone rang. It was my sister. She told me she and my brother were outside of our building, and my mom had locked herself in the apartment, closed all of the windows, and turned on the gas. She was going to kill herself.

I immediately snapped out of my coming-out induced haze and was horrified. I believed she could and would do it. That was the gravity of the news I had just given her. I called my aunts and asked them to come and help. I went to our apartment and pleaded for her to let me in. I promised her I would change. I promised her I would get help if she would just not kill herself. I would do whatever she wanted. Once again, my coming out was not about me but what I was doing to everyone else. At that moment, instead of coming to terms with the weight of what we had just discussed, I was consoling my mother, trying to keep her from ending her life.

The next day, I got home from work and found my Nextel phone lying on the dining room table. It had been completely crushed, and there was a hammer next to it. My mother walked in and told me my phone must have made me gay. I went into my bedroom, and my closet doors were wide open. All my clothes were gone—absolutely everything. I thought she might want me to move out, but when I went out to the building's trash area, I saw all of them in the dumpster with bleach poured over them. I returned to the apartment and asked her what happened, and she simply said my clothes were making me gay.

A few weeks later, she asked whether I would go with her to a "therapist." I agreed to go, still keeping my promise of trying to change who I was for her. The therapist specialized in gay conversion. I drove us, and as we approached, she pointed out the building we were going to. I knew then she had already been to see the therapist without me.

The doctor had his diplomas prominently displayed in his office, as well as pictures of himself and his wife and kids. The image of his family faced outward to the patient, not to him. I found that odd. It seemed like he was trying to prove a point to whoever sat across from him as opposed to having a gentle reminder of what awaited him at home every day. As soon as he opened his mouth, I knew why. He was gay gay gay.

"So, how long have you been this way?" he asked. His voice was relatively high-pitched, and his mannerisms and facial expressions were stereotypically gay.

"How long have *you* been this way?" I shot back.

"I don't know what you mean."

"Sure, I don't know what you mean either then."

"Your mom thinks we can fix you, and we certainly can. You have to want to be fixed, and in no time, you will be normal."

"I don't mind being fixed if it is fixable. But I have a question. Looking at your diplomas on the wall, if I were to call any of those schools and tell them you specialize in converting people like me from gay to straight, will you still be able to practice?"

It was as if a switch went off. He looked at my mother and said, "He's not the one that needs therapy; it's you. He doesn't want to be helped." He told me I was welcome to leave, and as I left the office, I couldn't help but say cheekily, "If you ever want to come to the other side, let me know!" My mom burst into tears, and I waited for her in the car. She cried the entire way home. I asked if she wanted to go back. She didn't answer me. We never discussed conversion therapy again.

Even though we were still reeling from the commotion my coming out had caused, we were united in keeping this as quiet as possible in the Armenian community and also from my father. Or at least, that is what I thought. One day, around 5:00 p.m. as I was wrapping up at work, a few of my friends from GALAS called me on my work phone and told me to tune into the Persian radio station. Every day, they had an advice segment where people called into the host for advice. Sort of like a radio version of a newspaper advice column. It was very popular in the Middle Eastern communities. As I turned it on, I heard two familiar female voices.

"My daughter and I just moved here from Iran. My oldest son moved here first. He had a major car accident at home, and my husband is back home. My son is supporting us, but we found out recently that he likes men."

The host told her I was sick, I needed a great deal of therapy, and if I crossed the line, my mother should throw me out of the house.

Unbeknownst to my mother, she had just outed me to the entire Armenian and Middle Eastern communities. Anyone who knew us knew of my accident and that I had just moved here. In a small community as homophobic as ours, word was going to travel like wildfire.

The next day, feeling gutted by having what was still a very personal truth broadcast over the radio, I went to my boss's sister's desk and asked whether I could talk to her for a moment. We had become good friends, and I figured I might as well come out to her too.

"I have to tell you something," I began.

"OK, what is it?" she responded eagerly.

"I'm gay."

"Is that it?"

"Yes."

"OK, how long have you known? Because I've known since we met."

She didn't care! For the first time, I came out to someone, and they didn't care. It was an immense relief, and exactly what I needed to feel like I had made the right decision to take control of my life. Maybe there was hope for acceptance and a normal life after all.

◇ ◇ ◇

I became the black sheep overnight. It took me twenty-one years to accept who I was; in fact, I still hadn't fully accepted who I was. How could I possibly expect my mother to accept me in twenty-one minutes? Sure, some mothers and fathers find out their children are gay and immediately wrap them in warm embraces and profess their pride in their child's bravery. But we were Armenian. We were from Iran. No matter how you sliced it, this wasn't going to go over well.

They weren't just homophobic; they were ignorant. Ignorant in the truest sense of the word. They didn't know what gay was. It was my responsibility to teach them. Albeit misguided, I appreciated that my mother sent me to therapy. It meant she thought this was a problem that could be solved. It wasn't a problem, and it couldn't be solved. But in making that effort, it showed me that she still cared. She could have, as many other Armenian families would have done, disowned me.

20. Dating (Boys)

A loving wife, two beautiful kids, and a hot boyfriend.
The American dream, right?

MY LIFE, AS I KNEW IT, was like a meticulously built house. Every experience, every relationship, every trial, came together to form this immensely complicated structure with a more confusing floorplan than anything I could ever hope to sell in my career. There were walls and locked doors everywhere, built out of compartmentalization and lies. In the center was me, and I was trapped. The only way to free myself was to take a wrecking ball to the whole damn thing and start afresh. That was coming out. The dust hadn't yet settled; the rubble was still scattered, but the real me had survived, and it was time to rebuild. I decided to start dating men.

I can still remember how uncomfortable I felt on my first real date with a man. We had met at a bar, and I thought he was incredibly attractive. But except for the couple at the movies, I had never seen two gay men interact as a couple in real life. I had seen two gay men interact sexually. But dating, that was always something I only did with women. I asked that we meet up in Silver Lake. It was just far enough from Glendale that I felt confident I wouldn't run into anyone who might know me. I arrived first and sat a table, my back turned to the entrance and facing a wall to ensure even if someone who knew me might show up, they'd see only the back of my head. Nobody knew me from that angle.

After my date showed up, we engaged in the typical small talk you expect on a first date. He asked me what I wanted out of life. My English was still a work in progress, but I was able to explain to him that I wanted children, I wanted to get married (to a woman), and I wanted to be able to sleep with men on the side. I can only imagine how confused he must have been. But when I think about that time, from a societal perspective, my difficulty in reconciling the fact I was gay with the fact I wanted to build a traditional life wasn't just because of my confusion. I *did* want those things sincerely. And back then, there was no indication they would be possible without a woman by my side. This was before #loveislove. Before the Andy Cohens and Neil Patrick Harrises of the world had put their family lives on the center stage and challenged the idea of what a family looked like. And even though I know now there were gay families out there somewhere paving the way for me, they were not living in Glendale. In Glendale, not only did you have to marry a person of the opposite sex if you wanted a family but that person needed to be Armenian. That was the way it was. I didn't realize I had a choice. In Iran, societal and cultural expectations trumped personal choices. And even as a newly out gay man, separating those cultural expectations from my consciousness was going to take time. In fact, despite feeling like a hero of sorts to the gay community after coming out, this inner conflict took a toll on me. I started to second-guess whether I could do this. I started to second-guess whether it was all worth it. After all, my mother was a mess, and I couldn't see a world in which my living life as an out gay man didn't bring hurt and shame to the people around me. I had struggled my entire life with questions about my sexuality. I was now in a completely new place where I could be a different person. Why would I simply confirm their suspicions and bring about the torment I had tried so desperately escape? I knew that, even after coming out, I could take it back. My family and community would accept me if I just told them it was all a big mistake and planned a huge Armenian wedding with some woman. I still was not sure if living honestly was truly worth it.

I didn't realize it yet, but moving to the US was, somewhat unbeknownst to me, allowing me to progress toward a world where who I was and what I wanted in life could actually coexist. I do not doubt that, if I had stayed in Iran, I would have married an Armenian woman, had children, slept with men on the side, and been miserable. Or perhaps I would have been blissfully ignorant living a double life. I don't know. But I do know life is much better when you lead it in truth and light. By the way, it must be said: to the guy who took me out on my first date, I'm sorry I wasn't ready yet!

Big smile on my face after mom had finally accepted me for who I am.

◇ ◇ ◇

I can't help but think how interesting it is that you can change so many aspects of your environment. You can change your clothes. You can find new friends, a new girlfriend, a new home. You can even move to a different country. But until you deal with what's inside and accept who you are and move on from a place of honesty, you are destined to repeat the same things over and over again. I had to learn how to accept myself. I was never ever going to get anywhere honest or authentic in life until I accepted who I was fully.

21. Falling in Love

It must be said, late-night pizza is always
a good decision. It changed my life.

WHEN I WAS TWENTY-ONE years old and had been in the US for a year and a half, my father came to America for another visit. This was my father's first visit since I had come out, and the prospect that he might find out mortified me. Would my mother, aunt, grandmother—or any of the other numerous Armenians who knew—tell my father I was gay? After all, my sexuality was now a completely open secret. There is the saying that what you do in the dark will always come to light. Well, it already had. The question now was what my father would do if and when he was brought into the light. I am not exaggerating when I say I was fearful for my life.

As I tried my absolute best to keep this massive bomb from dropping on my father and destroying everything in its wake, my father had a plan of his own. And, unfortunately, it was all about me. For the past year and a half, I had been the breadwinner. I started off supporting myself (with some help from my parents), and now I was supporting a family of four. I had a low-paying job. Our place was, to put it politely, very modest. Our lifestyle was the opposite of how we had lived in Iran, with Mercedes cars and designer clothes. My father had come to try and get me to finally ask for his help and put this little experiment behind me. He offered to buy me a luxury car and give me a CEO position at one of his projects in exchange for my agreeing to move back to Iran. By now, he was developing condominiums, and he was willing to let me take charge of one of the properties he was building. I knew if I went back, I would be rich. I would be one of the most eligible bachelors in our community and have my pick of any wife. Superficially, it was an attractive proposition, if for no other reason than it would be easier in so many ways. But deep down, I knew that agreeing to go back would essentially be voluntary servitude. It would be like making a deal with the devil. I knew who my father was. I knew what he was capable of, and I was very well acquainted with his anger. His proposition was one of the oldest tricks in the book. It was a typical modus operandi among powerful men all over the world who used it as a means of control. Dangle something shiny in front of someone who needs it. Make it almost impossible for them to say no. And if they say yes, make sure they can never change their mind.

At the same time, I was trying to plant roots in America. I was enrolled at the Los Angeles Community College and had a 4.0 GPA. My goal was to transfer to the University of Southern California and enroll in dental school. I wanted to be a dentist, a respectable profession in my culture. I guess on some level it was also important to bring honor to myself within my community. I didn't put as much stock into the standards I had grown up with, but they were still there. Becoming a dentist would prove to myself that, despite life's detours, I was still the smart, capable, and driven person who had knocked his college entrance exam out of the park and had a bright future ahead of him.

While my father was visiting, I decided it was time for me to buy a car. The one I had purchased when I first arrived in the US was on its last leg, and now I was making a little bit of money, I thought there was no time like the present. I also thought it would be a great way to show my father I was able to make it on my own. He and I went to a Kia dealership where there was a pre-owned Jeep Cherokee for sale. It was a beige limited edition with leather interior, a CD player, sunroof, the works. I had always wanted an SUV, and this was my dream car! I told him I was going to buy it, and he said, "Absolutely not. Over my dead body. If you do it, I will never talk to you again." I am not sure why he felt so strongly about me not purchasing the car; perhaps he felt like it was one more thing tying me to a life away from him. Or maybe he was threatened by me being able to do something without his help. In any regard, at that moment, I realized it was high time I learned to be OK with going against my dad's word.

I drove him home, turned right around, and went back to the dealership, and traded in my old car for the Jeep the same day. I don't know what came over me. When I came home, I showed my brother and sister my new car, and they were so excited! It was a big deal. Big enough for them to run back inside and tell my father. We had plans to have dinner at my aunt's, which was a twenty-minute drive away. Once my father found out about the car, he became so angry that we got into an argument and he threatened to strike me. In what was one of the most defiant things I had ever done in my life, I moved backward and said, "Remember, you are not a US citizen, so you don't want to hit your kid. It won't go well for you." Surprisingly, it worked. He backed away. But he was furious, not only about the car but about my power move. He decided to walk to dinner and arrived an hour after we did. He had my uncle drive him home, and he didn't talk to me for the remaining two months he was visiting. On the bright side, this made it easier to keep from him the fact I was gay.

My father's departures always brought ease and a sense of relief to our home. It had always been that way. My mother spoke differently. She even cooked differently! When my father was around, the food was bland and flavorless (no salt allowed!). When he left, my mother asked us what we wanted for dinner. Sometimes she would make each of our requests in one day. Other times, she'd plan meals for the entire week, making sure we each got what we had asked for. She loved to serve others when she had a choice in the matter and was appreciated for doing so. It is a quality she passed on to me. If I am forced to help someone, I won't. If they don't ask, I go above and beyond.

With the dynamics of our family shifting with every one of his visits, my father's departures were probably a relief for him as well. In LA, he was a nobody. Even *I* was finding my voice and strength to stand up to him, and his control over us was slipping away. In Iran, especially by himself, he was important. He had politicians in his pocket and women in towns all over the Middle East where he did business. That made him feel like a big deal. If you were him, would you rather have spent time in a small apartment with a family, and son, in particular, who didn't give you the (undeserved) respect you'd spent your life searching for? Remember, my father's existence, his relationships, the way he treated others were all in service of his insecurities.

When I met my partner, he was the complete opposite of what I was looking for in many ways. For starters, he was brown, like me. Don't get me wrong; there was no self-loathing racial hang-up going on. I find brown men attractive. It was just that I was in America now, and I felt like I should be looking for the American Dream. You know, a quintessential Brad Pitt type. Blonde hair, blue eyes, pale skin. Super white. My partner also was too young; he was the same age as me, and I liked older men. I typically gravitated toward men who were at least ten years older than I was. I felt mature for my age and found I usually connected with other mature men.

As so many love stories begin, we met after a night of drinking. It was one of the few times I decided to completely let loose in West Hollywood and get wasted and dance my heart out. We ended our night at the Abbey, of course. At around 3:00 a.m., I went to the pizza place next door, which is still open to this day. I was with some of my friends, and he was with his. He had seen me at parties before and, thanks to some liquid courage, decided to approach me. I asked him where he was from, and his response was the tackiest comeback line ever. "For you, I could be from anywhere." But I never said I didn't like tacky. I took his cell phone and added my number. I gave him strict instructions to call me the next day at 10:00 a.m. The next day, 10:00 a.m. came and went. Then 11:00, 12:00, 1:00. With each passing hour, I became more and more enraged. How dare this person flirt with me and not have the decency to call me as he promised! At 4:00 p.m. the phone rang. I let him have it. I told him if we were going to know each other, he had better remember to do what he says he is going to do when it comes to me. He apologized and blamed it on his hangover. He told me he didn't even clearly remember meeting me. I didn't care. After I cooled off, we agreed to meet up that evening at 7:00 p.m. for an actual date. And, well, now that we are married with a few kids under our belt, it's safe to say it went well.

Young love.

After my partner and I started dating, I felt comfortable enough to bring him home and introduce him to my mother. I didn't introduce him as my boyfriend—that would obviously have not gone over well. I just introduced him as a *friend* who was there to help me with my homework. Inventive, right? How many gay men do you know who have introduced someone as their *special friend*? Whatever, she went along with it. As we sat in the living room, at the dining table working, my mother was in the kitchen making coffee. Thinking we had complete privacy, I snuck a kiss. When I looked around, I saw my mother standing in the doorway, staring at us. My stomach sank. The last thing I wanted was for my mother and me to get into some massive emotional, ideological fight about being gay in front of my new boyfriend. To my surprise, she simply said, "The coffee is ready," turned, and walked back to her bedroom. My partner was petrified. Because he was from a similar background, he knew how big of a deal this was. He nervously asked whether he should leave. I wasn't sure. Should he? I wanted him to stay.

Maintaining a relationship while living with my family was not easy. I slept in the living room on the floor in front of the fireplace. Every night when it was time for bed, I pulled out a mattress, sheets, and a pillow to make a makeshift bed, and every morning, I woke up and put it all away. I liked sleeping in the living room, as opposed to sharing a bedroom with one of my family members, because it was the only way I could have any privacy. The other two rooms were for my mother (and father when he was in town) and my siblings. My 10:00 p.m. curfew was still in full effect, so staying overnight at my boyfriend's place was never an option. Instead, I woke up at 4:00 a.m., drove to his apartment, snuggled with him for a little while, and then drove to work.

My partner and I were different. We came from different backgrounds and had different ways of approaching life. But we clicked right away. Our shared cultural understanding made it easier to understand each other in a way that I don't know I would have been able to find if I had ended up with an all-American Brad Pitt type. He was brown, and he came from the same sort of religious and cultural environment as I did. If what we were doing wasn't so weird and foreign to him, maybe it shouldn't be for me either. I could be open with him about my family, my father, our living situation, and my struggles with being gay. He understood it all. He could very easily have been with someone who didn't have any of these problems. He wasn't constrained with the same sort of family situation that I was. But instead, he chose to be with me. In the grand scheme of everything, it was a whirlwind romance, though it didn't feel that way. It felt comfortable, honest, and beautifully simple.

After only forty-seven days of dating, my partner asked me to move in with him. He saw my living situation with my family, sleeping every night on the floor. He knew I was miserable, and he knew I couldn't afford to move. I know the idea of moving in together so quickly is surprising and may make us seem like we were moving at lesbian—I mean, lightning—pace, but it was the right decision. It was his love and concern for me that motivated him to make the proposition. As is his nature (always measured, always thoughtful), he explained why he thought it would be a good idea for us, highlighting the benefits and the potential drawbacks. It was a little like a business presentation. I think he thought he needed to convince me. He was wrong. He even told me to take some time to think about it. I needed none. As it is my nature to make decisions quickly and go with my gut, I took about sixty seconds before saying, "HELL YES!" I wanted to move in that day. I was ready. I kept an old beat-up green suitcase in my car so I could stay at his place at a moment's notice. This was a moment's notice, and I intended to stay at his place.

Sometimes I wonder why I trusted him so quickly. At that moment, after finally coming to terms with the fact I was gay and there was a possibility I could have the life I thought was so impossible just a short while before, I thought about him pushing my wheelchair. I don't believe in love at first sight, despite how quickly I fell in love. I think love builds as you survive the challenges that come your way. Passion, chemistry, attraction—those are all things that may or may not lead to being open enough to pursue and receive love, but they aren't love. He made me feel comfortable and made me feel understood. We came from vastly different

Our first apartment.

145

backgrounds but similar cultures. I can't imagine anyone from a different culture having the empathy necessary to not only make me feel secure during all of the drama that followed my coming out but also make me feel like it was perfectly normal.

There was one catch to our new living arrangement: I was still responsible for supporting my family. If I moved out, my income was still earmarked for my family's needs. The financial burden made it so I wouldn't be able to pay any rent if we lived together. It didn't matter to him; he just wanted me there. He agreed to pay two-thirds of the rent, with his roommate (who was perfectly fine with me moving in) paying one-third. Once we moved in together, he gave me an American Express card. It was clear with a blue chip in the middle. It was one of the coolest things I had ever seen. He told me the balance was zero and I could use it for my gas and expenses. Mind you, despite his generosity, he was no sugar daddy. He was in school himself and generating no income. But I suppose that speaks to the level of kindness he exhibited in service of making it easy for us to continue our relationship. Within two weeks, I had maxed it out. If I had been him, I would have dumped me and ran for the hills! But he didn't.

I needed to figure out a way to pay off this debt while also meeting the financial obligations I had for my family. I decided it might be time to get a better-paying job. I applied for a job with Hilti, a prominent power tool manufacturer. If hired, I would be a Hilti representative, selling tools out of Home Depot and making $42,000 a year. More than I had ever made in my life. The job required me to take a test first, which I passed. After that, I was given an in-person interview. When I went in, the interviewer was impressed with my test scores, but he said I wasn't a strong enough communicator. My English was simply not good enough yet. I didn't get the job. I was extremely disappointed. I had already started thinking about what I would be able to do with the money. It would have been a significant bump in my salary and would have helped pay off the debt I had racked up. Of course, in hindsight,

I am so grateful I didn't get the job. It wasn't what I was meant to do. To this day, some eighteen years later, when I am having an off day, my partner will joke, "Do you want to go back to Hilti?" Definitely not.

One of my favorite cousins, who had been one of the few family members who were supportive of me coming out, happened to be dating a real estate agent. We got to know each other at family events and just by traveling in similar circles. He was a great guy. He was smart, had a witty and sarcastic sense of humor, and was very competitive. He was also successful. I admired him, and I shared that admiration with my partner. I had never *wanted* to be like anyone per se, until I met him. I knew he was what I wanted to be. His drive, his confidence, and his success were how I saw myself. I just wasn't sure how to get there.

At that point, I had no idea how exactly I was going to make ends meet. I was hoping to go to dental school, but that wasn't a sure thing, and even if it worked out, I wouldn't be making money for years. By then, I had quit my job at the carpet installer so I could focus on school. I had a small job at the school library, which I used, along with student loans, to help support my family. I also used financial aid to bridge the gap for tuition. I would often leave the library and go to a grocery store called Food for Less. They always had Top Ramen on sale. I ate about two packs a day. I didn't care about sodium back then. My partner helped me with other expenses and, of course, rent. He was mostly taking care of all of my needs, and I was taking care of my family's needs. I felt responsible for their well-being because I had brought them to the US from Iran.

My financial situation may have been typical for a college student; after all, you are supposed to be poor in college. But I knew it would not work for me. I had responsibilities to my family, and I couldn't expect them to sit and go without food for the years and years it would take to become a dentist. One experience drove that fact home. I went over to my old place for a visit, where my mom and siblings were still living. My sister and brother were sitting at a coffee table, doing their homework. My mom wasn't home at the time; she had taken a job at a local bakery shop and was out working.

I opened the refrigerator and saw a piece of bread, two eggs, and some milk. I thought, *If my mom is not home, it's past seven o'clock, and there is essentially no food in the house, what are my brother and sister going to eat?* I didn't live there anymore, and my boyfriend was providing my food and shelter. I didn't have any wants or needs. I was paying rent for my family, but I hadn't made it a priority to check up on them. I felt devastated and guilty about what I saw. I left and, using my partner's credit card, went to Burger King—a family favorite. I bought Whoppers, onion rings, French fries, the whole nine yards. My mom eventually came home, and we all ate together. This was an excellent solution for that night, but I had to figure out something long term.

The next morning, I drove to my cousin's boyfriend's (well, by then, he was her ex-boyfriend) real estate office at seven o'clock. He showed up about thirty minutes later, even though his office didn't open until nine. He asked me what I was doing there. I told him I needed a job, and he politely told me there wasn't a job there for me. Déjà vu, right? He was a single father and had children; I knew he could use help in some capacity. I offered to pick up his dry cleaning or wash his car. Whatever he needed. He declined. The next day, I showed up again and asked for a job. Once again, he declined. On the third day, I showed up with Starbucks and donuts for his staff. This time, he invited me to his office, and with his loud and boisterous disposition, he agreed to give me a job as a messenger.

My job was basically to do whatever needed to be done on a daily basis. I put up signs and collected them. I dropped off disclosures and envelopes. I picked up lockboxes, all of it. The job paid $2,000 a month. After he hired me, I left his office in tears. So many jobs that I had applied for had rejected me; finally, I had a real job making real money. I wanted to celebrate. I called my boyfriend and told him I would be late and went to pick up my mom and siblings. I told them

I had just gotten a new job, and I was taking them out to the nicest restaurant I knew, Baja Fresh. At Baja Fresh (a Chipotle-esque fast-casual restaurant) you could get tacos, a burrito bowl, and salads. They had an incredible selection of sauces. It was, to me, fine dining. When we arrived, my mom was confused. How could we afford this? I told her, "Mom, I got a new job, and from this moment on, you never have to worry about money again. I make so much money!" I came home on cloud nine. Ever the intuitive man, I think my happiness planted a seed in my partner's head.

A few weeks later, on a perfectly normal day, I came home to find my partner waiting with a huge box of books for me. They were real estate manuals. We had never talked about real estate, but on a leap of faith, he bought them and asked whether I had ever thought about getting my license. At first, I was resistant. In the Armenian community, almost everyone had a real estate license. It was almost like a joke. It wasn't a respectable profession in Armenian culture and was akin to being a car salesman. Even though my boss was a real estate agent, he had reached a level of success that seemed both unattainable and atypical. While I saw his business acumen and success as an inspiration, I didn't think I would get to that level as a real estate agent. Everyone was just trying to strike a deal and make a little extra money on the side.

I looked at my partner and said pointedly, "You have a master's degree. In my culture, you don't date people who are not on the same level as you are. Why would you want to be with someone uneducated? I am going to school to be a dentist, and now you are telling me you think I should quit? You don't want me to have an education?"

"Education isn't just about school. Look at your experiences. Look at what you have been through. You have an education." He seemed so confident.

I wasn't sure whether he was right. I had always been insecure that he was more educated than I was and felt deep down I was not good enough for him. He had come from a well-to-do family in comparison to my own. I thought becoming a dentist would put us at a more level playing field. Being a real estate agent . . . not so much. Nonetheless, I trusted him. I believed that he believed in me, and so I decided to do it. I decided to get my real estate license. Looking back, this was a pivotal moment in our relationship. One that made me fall deeper in love with him and set the stage for the dynamic of our union for years to come. He pushed me to dream bigger and work toward a success that was tailored to who I was, not who my parents or my community thought I should be. He made me feel accountable to myself and held me to a standard that made me want to deliver for myself. For the first time in my life, I was working hard because of my own ambitions, not others' expectations. In many ways, he was like a parental figure. He gave me the love and support I needed to become my best self. I needed to grow, learn, explore, and take risks. I knew, no matter what, I would be OK.

As time progressed, I made a point to take on more and more responsibility and try to make a name for myself at work. My boss was receptive to it, but my coworkers were envious of the attention I was getting. One of my female coworkers had it out for me. She was a bit of a poser, so we can call her "the Poser." The Poser claimed to have been a doctor in her old country, but now she was a real estate agent. She led a very glamorous life; she drove the nicest car and wore the nicest clothes, and she really made an impression when she walked in. The odd thing was that, in a real estate office, it is not difficult to know what other people are bringing home. It's based on what you are selling. It was obvious the lifestyle she led was not in line with her success at the company.

One day, I was cleaning the office after everyone left for the evening, and the phone rang. The phone systems were all connected, so if you pushed #2013 on any desk phone in the office, it would connect you to the main line. I just happened to be emptying the trash can by the Poser's desk when the phone rang, so I answered it. As I was hanging up, she walked in and caught me on her phone. She looked at me and said, "Do not ever touch my desk or my phone. I don't want to get HIV from you." That experience left an impact on me. I started to think Glendale may not be the place for me. I was tired of always feeling like an outsider. I was tired of feeling gratitude for basic kindness and respect. I went to the boss's office and told him that I was thinking about moving on. He pushed back.

"How much would it take you to stay?" he asked.

"Twenty-two hundred dollars?" I said, not entirely sure what I was worth.

"Are you sure? You don't think you deserve more?" he responded.

"If you think I deserve more, then you should give me more, but it isn't up to me."

I have always been of the opinion (and have brought this view to my own leadership roles) that an employee should never have to ask for a raise or play any sort of guessing game when it comes to their value. When it comes to raises, either an employee has earned it and their boss will give it to them, they haven't earned it and they need to be more realistic about their value, or they have earned it but their boss isn't paying attention and thus is a poor leader and they should find an environment with better leadership. Nonetheless, to keep me there, my boss was trying to either reveal to me what he thought I was capable of or get me to open my eyes and realize it for myself. I suppose it depends on how you look at it.

He continued, "I think you should be making twenty-five thousand a month."

"Nobody makes twenty-five thousand a month!" I said, shocked by the suggestion.

"You don't see yourself making twenty-five thousand a month? I promise you that you can. I see it. You should get your license."

"Well, I am studying for my exam," I revealed.

"Well, once you finish, we are going to transition you."

Then he gave me some of the best advice I have ever received. It's actually rather unconventional in the real estate world. He told me if I started working with him, I was never ever allowed to sell a home owned by a family member or friend, or he would fire me. I told him it wouldn't be hard for me because all of my friends were broke and my family hated me. In retrospect, what he was trying to teach me with this rule was that to be a truly successful real estate broker, you have to sell homes to people you don't know. He was teaching me how to fish as opposed to waiting for fish to come to me.

Now, when I coach other real estate agents, I always say the same thing: *Think of all the people you know and put them in a box. Now think of all of the people you don't know and put them in a box. Which box is bigger? If you sell homes only to people you know, you will be making only as much as they make.* My experience with representing family and friends is they often don't respect your expertise, want to run the show, and even ask for commission back (as a discount). When you work with any customer, that customer should value the work you put in for what it is worth. When you work with any customer, they should value your expertise as a seasoned professional and hire you for that reason, not as a favor to you. Often, family members give you business out of entitlement, not because of your qualifications. My broker knew that no family gives a realtor business because they are good; they give them business out of obligation. My broker wanted me to believe I was going to be so good, I would be able to get business based on my merits. I believed him. He was my mentor and idol. I copied everything he did. I ate the same salads he ate and drank the same Perrier. I took my coffee the same way. I even wanted to buy the same car he drove after I had made it. I saw myself and my future in him. Except for one thing: he loved to play the piano. I couldn't bring myself to touch a piano.

Now my studying (which had been ongoing since my boyfriend talked me into it) was accompanied by a sense of purpose and optimism that hadn't been there before. I started to believe my boyfriend was right—maybe this was the path I belonged on. I was very confident in my ability to ace the math portions of the test; after all, I had taken Calculus 3 in high school. But I knew my English skills weren't necessarily where they needed to be, and I would need some help on the vocabulary questions. I took a crash course on word association, which helped me to take whatever words were in a particular question and, through association, figure out what the most probable answer was based on the strongest association. Every time I took a practice exam, I compared my answers with the correct answers and used word association to commit the relationship to memory. As the Dalai Lama says, when you talk, you are only repeating what you already know. But if you listen, you may learn something new.

I wasn't required to take a course; I simply self-studied for two months. Weeks later, the results were in, and I had passed! My boyfriend cooked for me to celebrate the occasion. We were ecstatic.

◇◇◇

In working for my cousin's ex, I learned it really takes only one person to believe in you to change the entire trajectory of your life. He believed I was capable of much more than I thought I was. He taught me to let go of the preconceived notions I had about honorable professions and see my potential and my ultimate calling. My partner also believed in me when I didn't. He pushed me to get comfortable being uncomfortable.

22. Career Takeoff

Maybe there are good cults out there too?

THE FIRST HOME I EVER SOLD was on Christmas Eve. It was a condo project that my boss had almost completely sold out. It was typical for him to give me whatever last remaining units were left after a project had almost sold out. Even though I would have loved to open my own project, I never complained. After all, it was experience. A younger woman came to the open house and told me she had recently broken up with her boyfriend, who was unwilling to commit to buying a home with her for a reason that hit pretty close to home. Her ex-boyfriend was gay. As we spoke, I made a wise business decision not to tell her I also was gay. It was best I kept that to myself. She told me she was ready to find something on her own. She didn't need a man (especially a man who liked other men). I played it cool and told her to take a look around the condo to see if she liked it and then we could go for dinner afterward. She loved the unit, and our conversation over dinner helped to seal the deal. Afterward, I felt inspired by my ability to gain her trust so quickly.

I thought about how much time I had spent trying to please other people by studying to go to dental school. The idea of being a dentist had never excited me the way that one sale did. From then on, I made it my mission to know every single unit on the market. Even if a particular property wasn't in a condo project we were selling, I knew what our competition was. I knew which units had the best views, what the homeowners associations dues were for every building, which buildings had parking, specific floorplans based on a unit's position within a building, and even school districts. I knew it all. Eventually, I was the condo expert buyer's agent for my market, and during my very first year, I sold seventeen units. All while still working as my boss's assistant.

One of the interesting things about my boss's business model was he didn't seek out the most expensive properties. Often when you think of successful real estate agents, you think of the agents who sell the insanely expensive mansions that bring in astronomical commissions. He didn't do that. There was a time when a prominent Armenian family contacted our office, wanting him to sell their home. I picked up the phone while my boss was out of the office and they gave me their information. When I printed out the title sheet, I realized it was a single-family home in one of the fanciest areas of Glendale and worth well over a million dollars. I gave it to my boss and was excited and hopeful he would give me an opportunity to host an open house for it and potentially pick up some wealthy buyer leads. He called them up, thanked them for their inquiry, and explained to them that he didn't sell single-family homes and then gave them two referrals. I was shocked. Even if given the opportunity to sell an expensive home, he turned it down in favor of selling condominiums.

I struck up the nerve to ask him why. It seemed like he was throwing money away. He told me that it wasn't for the money. He wasn't interested in getting one huge commission every once in a while. Instead, he was interested in being the top-producing agent in his area. He wanted to be known as the guy who sold all the condos in the area. It was then I learned that top-producing agents do not work for the money; they work for prominence in the market. It is the only way to secure market share and create longevity in your career.

During that first year, I was able to pay off all the debt I had racked up by using my partner's credit card and from a failed Yahoo Store venture. Prior to my real estate job, I had gone into business with a friend, and his father lent us $32,000 to buy products to sell on Yahoo. It was a colossal failure. Even though my friend's father never asked for the money back, I never forgot I had this cloud of debt hanging over me. As soon as I was able, I went to him and gave him a check for $32,000 plus interest (as determined by me). He was confused as to why I paid him back for the entirety and not just half (given that he'd loaned the sum to the both of us). I told him he was entitled to all of it. He was grateful and appreciated my desire to do the honorable thing.

My partner had student loans of nearly $30,000, and I paid those off as well. They weren't mine, but he had given me so much and supported me in every way imaginable. I felt I owed it to him. I took my brother to an orthodontist and got him braces for $6,200, which I paid in three installments. I continued to pay all of my family's expenses. It felt amazing, but after making almost $150,000 my very first year, I was broke. I also hadn't learned about Uncle Sam. As a real estate agent, it's your responsibility to account for taxes when you receive commissions so you can pay income tax come tax season. I didn't know that. My second year of selling real estate, I filed my taxes and realized how much I had to pay. I was making money, but I hadn't learned the business. Eventually, I was shopping at Food for Less for Top Ramen again. I knew it was time to hire a coach to teach me how to bring in more business. His name was Mike Ferry, and his services cost $1,000. I didn't have the money to pay him, but I knew if I paid the minimum payment on my credit card, the payment would go through (even if it left me over my limit.) I thought it was a necessary expense—one last financial gamble in the interest of having the means to never make them in the future.

My coach started working with me on generating more business. He believed strongly in cold-calling for prospective clients, so we did. Every Armenian person I called said the same thing: "I have a real estate license already; my son has a real estate license too. My wife is an agent. If I let you sell my house, how much will you charge me?"

They were all nonstarters. How could I develop more business if every potential customer immediately started our conversations by asserting the fact they didn't really need my help unless it was for a discount? I knew it was time to move beyond Glendale—and sadly, beyond the brokerage where I'd gotten my start. Discreetly, I began interviewing.

My boyfriend and I had been living in West Hollywood for a while, and I was commuting nearly twenty-five miles to Glendale and back every day. If you know anything about the infamous Los Angeles traffic, you know twenty-five miles a day is legitimate torture. The natural decision was to start exploring brokerages closer to home.

I interviewed in Beverly Hills at an extremely prestigious brokerage. The owner was regarded as one of the top agents in the city. Her clientele was the cream of the crop. Actors, singers, executives, you name it—they all bought or sold with her. Her office epitomized the glamour and opulence you would expect from one of the most successful agents in one of the most wealthy and well-to-do zip codes in the world. She was just as glamorous. We sat down in her office, and she looked at me in a way that made me feel exposed and insecure.

"Do you speak Farsi?" she asked.

"Yes."

"Well, it's very hard to work with Persians. I could give you all of the smaller deals for two or three million dollars . . ." she said with a matter-of-fact tone.

I was so intimidated by the proposition. Those were not small deals in my world, and I was unsure whether the prospect of working in an environment in which others viewed them as small deals was the right fit for me. We ended our meeting, and I made my way out. As I was leaving the office, the owner's daughter, who also worked there, complimented my tie and asked where it was from. Not missing a beat or giving me an opportunity to respond, she flipped it over to look at the brand. It was DKNY, and I had purchased it from Ross Dress for Less. She looked at me with such disapproval. It made my skin crawl.

It was one of the most beautiful things I owned and yet clearly not good enough in comparison to their glamorous dress code. A lot of my clothes were from Ross. I liked Ross. I didn't fit in at this brokerage. I felt like a high school kid who wasn't good enough to sit with the cool kids at the lunch table. I left and never followed up.

I decided to take my pursuits to the San Fernando Valley. Studio City, to be exact. A healthy yet more accessible market. I interviewed with a huge company that was all about numbers but with very little heart. My "interview" was primarily about what splits they offered as opposed to whether I was a fit for the company. I immediately got the impression that it was a sink or swim kind of environment. It didn't feel right, either. I was running out of companies to interview with and feeling discouraged. Maybe Glendale was where I belonged?

As I continued to search for the right brokerage, feeling less optimistic by the day, some of my industry friends who knew I was looking gave me some advice. Whatever you do, don't go to Keller Williams. It was a new company, and everyone made fun of it. I heard it over and over again. They described the culture as something between church and a cult. Nobody understood the model. It was nontraditional, and in real estate, nontraditional was not good. I heeded their advice and steered clear.

Eventually, I joined a big-box company called RE/MAX that was nationally renowned. I was so impressed with their vibe. When I pulled up in my convertible, there was valet service. The office was in a beautiful building. It felt just fancy enough without making me feel out of place. I felt at home immediately. After a short interview, I was on board. I wrote a $2,000 check for errors and omissions insurance, which is liability insurance for agents, and finally felt my search had come to an end. I was confident I had finally found where I belonged. As I was leaving, I saw several agents who were walking with boxes. I asked whether they were moving in, excited that I wasn't the only one who felt like this was the right place to hang their license. It was a trend!

They told me that they weren't moving in; they were moving out. The office was consolidating. Confused, I referenced my dictionary (which means I called my boyfriend) and asked what "consolidating" meant. He told me that it meant shutting down. I parked my car, ran back up into the office, and found my check exactly where I had left it. I snatched it and ran.

When I got back downstairs, I asked one of the agents where he was heading. He told me he was going to the new company across the street, Keller Williams. My stomach sank. Should I follow him? I had no other prospects. But I really didn't want to work for them after hearing such terrible things. I thought it meant I wasn't good enough to get into a brokerage people respected. But I had already quit working for my boss in Glendale. Begrudgingly, I walked to Keller Williams and decided to try to meet with the managing broker.

The environment was eerily calm and relaxed. Unlike any other brokerage I had visited before. The manager was sitting and eating nuts. He was friendly.

"Hi, can I help you?" he said cheerily.

"I am looking for a company, and I need to know what you can offer. I made two hundred twenty-five thousand dollars last year, and I want to know what you can do for me."

By then, I had a bit of an ego. I already thought I was better than the company. I was also tired of looking and just wanted to bypass the pleasantries and get down to business.

"Do you want to have sushi with me? It's lunchtime, and I'm hungry," the manager said.

It was an odd invitation, but I agreed. We walked together to a sushi place in the same complex. We sat for nearly two and a half hours. During that time, I told him my life story. I told him where I was from, about my accident, how I had moved to the US, all the odd jobs I had worked, and how I eventually found my way to real estate. He didn't say a single word until the very end, when he told me we had to make sure we hit $225,000 to prove I could still produce in a new environment. I was sold. Not because the splits were especially wonderful—they were 70/30 (pretty standard). I also had to pay an office fee. But the fact he took a vested interest in me and truly believed I could be successful made me feel like this was exactly the type of supportive environment I needed to begin the next chapter of my real estate career. I moved in the same day.

Starting in a new market was not as easy as I had hoped it would be. After nearly four months, I hadn't sold a single house. I started to question my decision and even considered going back to Glendale. Had I been too cavalier to think my success would translate? Every week that went by without a transaction chipped away at my confidence and the hubris I had when I initially had my meeting with Keller Williams. Fearing my lack of success would also start to erode the confidence my manager had in me when he first brought me on, he and I sat down for a conversation. I think he sensed I was feeling discouraged. Rather than reprimand me and tell me to shape up or ship out—or worse, be completely unattached and content to watch me crash and burn—he made a point to tell me not to give up and he would not have brought me on if he wasn't confident I could succeed. That little vote of confidence was all I needed. I started working even harder. I did absolutely everything I could to drum up business. I knocked on doors, sent even more postcards, and made even more cold calls. It worked. By the end of the year, I was the office's top producer.

◇ ◇ ◇

Joining Keller Williams taught me just how crucial being in the right environment with the right people is to a successful business. It can make or break you. No matter what level you work at, whether you are just starting out or are one of the most successful in your field, having a mentor—or in my case, a coach—is often the best way to maintain accountability. Having a coach keeps me on track and ensures I don't get complacent. Don't let others get in your head and dictate what is best for you based on their opinions. If I had listened to everyone else, I would never have even stepped foot in Keller Williams. It ended up being one of the best professional decisions I have ever made.

23. Success at Keller Williams

I was gay, brown, and an immigrant. English was not
my first language, and I spoke with an accent. I couldn't
change it, so everyone would have to get over it.

AROUND THE SAME TIME I moved to Keller Williams, my partner
made a significant career shift and left the job he had been at since
he finished graduate school. I cautioned him against it. I thought
it was better to be a big fish in a small pond rather than trying
to make a name for himself at a massive corporation. Thank God
he didn't take my advice. It proved to be the smartest decision he
ever made and changed his career trajectory, and our lives, forever.
It has always struck me as ironic that our career successes seemed
to occur if not simultaneously then very close together. In some
relationships, one successful partner can make another successful
partner feel jealous or inferior. That has never been a problem for
us. Neither of us would ever want to make the other feel guilty for
succeeding—quite the contrary.

I have always wanted my partner to reach the absolute highest degree
of his potential, and I am sure he would say the same thing for me. He
motivates me to rise to the occasion. Not because we are competitive
with one another but because we strive to motivate one another. I believe
the true test of a healthy relationship is whether that person brings out
the best in you. My partner most definitely brings out the best in me.

About a year after joining Keller Williams, the owner of the office offered me a promotion of sorts. He asked whether I would be willing to sign on as an assistant manager. I had no idea what an assistant manager did. He explained I would report to my manager, the man who had hired me, and be responsible for helping the office to grow by recruiting new agents and providing guidance to new team members. The additional responsibilities paid $30,000, and I was still allowed to continue my own transactions. I couldn't see any reason why I wouldn't be willing to take on extra responsibilities for an additional $30,000 a year. I told the owner I was interested. Many years later, he became a very close friend and mentor who was instrumental in shaping my career at Keller Williams.

Before I could officially be hired as an assistant manager, I had to take an Activity Vector Analysis (AVA). It was a behavioral assessment that our company, along with many others, used to assess a candidate's natural inclinations to help determine whether they were suitable for whatever position they were up for. The owner's assistant sent me a link, and I took it on my computer.

Once the owner received the results, he asked me to meet with him in his Hollywood Hills office on Sunset Boulevard. His office was a penthouse in a gorgeous building. The glass walls provided sweeping views of the city. We met in the conference room and sat at an enormous conference table. It was big enough to seat dozens, but for this meeting, it was just the two of us. The expansive and beautiful space juxtaposed with the intimate nature of just the two of us meeting made the experience all the more intimidating. Sitting a few feet away, he pulled out my AVA results and explained, "So, your assessment says you are only a thirty-four percent match to the qualities we are looking for in an assistant manager. Essentially, that means you aren't going to be a good one. You will be too blunt, too opinioned, insubordinate, and controlling."

By the time he finished, my intimidation had given way to anger. I sat, hands crossed and lips pursed. Why did he bring me all the way out here to tell me I was going to suck at the job? I wasn't going to just sit there in silence and let him insult me.

"Look, I made seven hundred forty thousand dollars this year. I am an amazing agent. Do you think I need your thirty-thousand-dollar-a-year assistant manager job?" I shot back.

"Don't get upset! We ran your behavior assessment for a different role! Instead of the assistant manager, we ran you for the manager role, and you were a ninety-nine-percent match."

Well, his reassurance was exactly what I needed to hear to turn the entire mood of the conversation around instantly. I started to smile, ego safely in place.

"Would you be interested in a manager position? Before you answer, I want to remind you that, as a manager, you won't be able to conduct transactions," he said.

"No. Absolutely not. I won't take a position if I can't sell real estate. I have to sell real estate."

"Well, wait a second." He tried to get me back into the conversation. "You can conduct transactions, just not in the same market. You aren't allowed to manage a team you are competing with. It's a conflict of interest, and they will think you are taking their market share," he explained.

"I would never do that! I would want to help them, not compete with them." I was offended just by the suggestion.

Nonetheless, the rule wasn't a reflection of my character or trustworthiness but simply a check to prevent any manager from alienating his team or, worse, taking advantage of them. More importantly, it was nonnegotiable. If I wanted to be a manager, I would have to manage an office other than the one I sold houses from. At the time, he was considering opening an office in Calabasas, a suburb in the Valley. Everyone knows Calabasas now, largely as the result of the Kardashian family. But back then, it was a pretty sleepy suburb. Wealthy, *sure*, but not carrying the kind of cachet it does now. I knew nothing about

Calabasas and generally felt like this job opportunity was not for me. I wanted to turn it down then and there, but we agreed to table the discussion and pick it up later.

As time passed, I let the idea of being a manager fade into the background and continued doing what I was good at—selling real estate. A few months later, the owner I had met with in the Hollywood Hills reached out again to let me know he had decided against opening an office in Calabasas. I wasn't terribly disappointed. Even though the opportunity wasn't going to move forward, he still made sure to reiterate his strong belief I would make a great manager. He referred me to the owner of another Keller Williams office in Los Angeles. Thinking he may be on to something, I decided it wouldn't hurt to take another meeting.

The owner of this office loved me and agreed I would make a strong leader—but not for his office. His reasoning was it was an older market, I was only twenty-five years old, and he was unsure whether agents would be receptive to reporting to someone so much younger. He didn't say it, but I also could tell he wasn't comfortable hiring a gay man to manage a fairly conservative market in LA. I felt a bit like a soccer ball as that owner kicked me over to another owner who was in the process of opening a new office in Encino, a different suburb in the Valley. We met, and once again, we clicked. But I didn't hear back from him for months.

When I finally heard back from the Encino owner, he explained they had decided against opening the office entirely. However, he co-owned an office in Sherman Oaks. It was not doing well, and they were considering new management. A group of three people owned it, and they all wanted to meet with me.

Once again, I prepped for an interview. At this point, I could practically do it in my sleep. By the time we finally sat down for the interview, it was clear my reputation had preceded me. Unfortunately, it wasn't the positive aspects of my reputation (at least, they weren't positives to the owners). They had already heard my English wasn't strong, I was gay, and I was very new to real estate. I was already running at a deficit when I walked into the room. Yet again, I was told I was not the right fit. This time, for the Sherman Oaks market. Well, actually, they left me hanging and told me they didn't intend to move very fast. Anyone who has ever interviewed for a job knows what that means . . . no.

Throughout this time of interviews and false starts, I had the opportunity to meet leaders and owners from across the company. I realized managing others was something I not only would be good at but something I loved. I even paid out of pocket to attend a leadership conference in Austin to learn more about the role. My initial hesitance had done a complete 180. I wanted to be a leader. The more rejection I experienced, the more I wanted it. Also, as a salaried position, it appealed to me as it would provide a bit of much-needed financial security. Even though I was making a lot of money in commission, I was also spending a lot of money to further my business and support my family. I was struggling financially.

Not willing to give up the idea, I felt the Sherman Oaks office was my best shot. Even though they told me they were not going to decide anytime soon, I decided to not take no for an answer (a tactic that had served me well so far). I created a PowerPoint presentation with a six-month, one-year, and three-year action plan for Sherman Oaks and took it to the owners' office—unannounced. They were not happy to see me. They reminded me they were not planning to hire a manager anytime soon and told me to go home. I refused. I asked them to just listen to me. I told them they couldn't afford not to. I knew they were losing tens of thousands of dollars a month. They couldn't afford to move slowly. There is a famous saying: *good things come to those who wait.* I couldn't agree less. Good things come to those who go after them. Whatever is left goes to those who wait.

Swayed, they let me into the office, and we all sat down in the boardroom. I explained my plan to them. There was already an existing manager in the Sherman Oaks office. I told them they didn't need to fire her or throw her out. Instead, they should move her to an agent position and make her a mentor. She was currently making $150,000 per year, and if they moved her out of the manager role and put me in her place, I would ask for only $70,000 per year. I was willing to take the financial hit for security. The way I saw it, if I moved into a managerial role and was still selling real estate, it would be at a net positive. If, for some reason, my real estate business didn't survive, I was still guaranteed enough money to make ends meet. This meant enough money to make sure my mother was taken care of. I could buy my own food and pay for my own car and not have to burden my partner with my personal expenses.

They took the bait. They agreed to my plan and also agreed to pay me an extra $10,000 more than I asked for. The grand total came to $80,000 a year. As a vote of confidence, I offered to write them a check for $80,000 and gave it to them. At the end of the year, if I didn't meet my goals, I gave them permission to cash the check and pay themselves back for what they had spent on me. If I met my goals, they would have to tear up the check. They were impressed by my confidence (and intrigued by the financial upside of practically splitting their managerial expenses in half). What business owner would say no? The current manager was underperforming, so if I performed poorly, it would simply leave them where they were, but for $80,000 cheaper. If I did well, they would reap the rewards and still have saved $80,000. It was a win-win.

The Sherman Oaks office was $217,000 in debt when I came on board. There were about forty agents, and none of them produced except for one—the previous manager. The office was roughly eighteen hundred square feet on the second floor of a high-rise building with old carpet and only one bathroom. There was no parking, no signage, no nothing. I had inherited a mess. And I was ecstatic. I was a manager! It was sort of like when an eighteen-year-old leaves the comforts of their parents' home to go live in a dorm room. One would think the luxuries of mom's cooking, your own big bed, and a nice bathroom to yourself would trump sharing a bedroom with a stranger and a bathroom with dozens of strangers. But it didn't. Why? Because of independence. Because of the responsibility. I was out on my own, and the Sherman Oaks office presented a challenge that invigorated me. I was ready for the challenge.

Taking this giant leap was a life lesson. Failure simply wasn't an option. When you burn all your bridges, you have to make the island home. There was no going back for me. This had to work. I had burned the bridge with my original broker who discovered me in Glendale by leaving him and then later competing with him. I had even burned the bridge with my first manager at Keller Williams, who believed in me like no one ever had before. Eventually, once we had grown up a bit, we became friends again, and we continue to have love and respect for one another. But back then, we were also competing for the same pool of agents, and it was scrappy. Most important of all, I had told my partner I believed I could be successful in this new role and market. If I failed, disappointing him would be the most difficult part of it all.

When I started, I made it clear on day one to my new team that it didn't matter what I sounded like, how good my English was, where I came from, or what I did in my personal life. Absolutely none of it mattered unless it had to do with producing. We were going to make this work. We were going to turn this office around. I pulled the former manager aside, whose job I had taken, and expressed how important I thought it was that she stay on with me. She reluctantly stayed but didn't seem especially inclined to trust I would be better at her job than she had been. She was a tough cookie. I added earning her respect to my growing list of goals.

I dove headfirst into recruiting efforts. We needed more agents. The more agents we had, the more likely we were to turn a profit. This proved a bit difficult. I had forgotten how important the environment had been for me when I was searching for a brokerage. If I had interviewed at the Sherman Oaks office with its musty carpet and stale air, I probably would have said, "Thank you, but absolutely not." Recruits had trouble finding our office when they came for interviews. There were a number of our competitors on the first floor of our office building. Naturally, recruits assumed we would be in the same vicinity. Kind of like when you see a McDonalds, Burger King, and Wendy's all clustered together. I had to explain to them that we were actually the Subway, a bit of a trek down the road. We were the little tiny door on the second floor that you could miss if you blinked while walking by. I persisted. I didn't have a choice.

One of the best things (and there were many) of becoming a manager was the education. Keller Williams invested in my education. Given that I hadn't gone to business school, it was invaluable. I learned about recruiting, retention, budgets, staying on budget, income, other income, succeeding through others, delegation, rewarding, and team-building and culture. I learned it was never about how much you made but rather how much you kept, a lesson that would have served me well in my previous years as an agent. I learned giving things away was not the way to recruit; rather, you had to show value. For example, instead of decreasing your splits, show why your brokerage deserved the splits they asked for. If someone came for money, they would leave for money.

Not long after signing on as manager of the Sherman Oaks office, we all went to Atlanta for Keller Williams's annual awards ceremony and conference. It was the first ceremony I had ever attended. Awards at the ceremony were given out by region, and I was excited to see who won from my region, the Central Southern Region.

I was elated when I heard "Now, the Central Southern Region's Number-One Agent in Gross Commission Income, Harma Hartouni!" booming over the loudspeakers. It was for the $740,000 of income I had generated as an agent in the prior year. It felt as if I had won an Academy Award for my first-ever performance. About twenty minutes later, after they had finished announcing all the awards, they began announcing promotions.

Once again, booming over the loudspeaker, I heard my name. "We are pleased to announce our new leadership group that will be serving our region, with team leader Harma Hartouni!" Everyone who had just cheered for my success twenty minutes earlier was dumbfounded by this significant shift in my career trajectory. Allow me to explain. Taking a leadership role is typically something people do when they don't want to do transactions. It abided by the adage, "Those who can't do, teach." Being an agent wasn't easy. It required you to build a business with its very own customer base. A lot of people weren't good at it. A lot of people didn't want to be bothered with the volatility and uncertainty associated with it. Conventional wisdom was that if you *were* good at it, then you counted your lucky stars and got out there and sold! A gross commission income of $740,000 in one year meant I was damn good at it. At that moment, with everyone looking confused and bewildered at the announcement, I summoned every bit of strength I could muster to excuse myself and run to the closest bathroom stall. I broke down in tears. Not happy tears. Everyone out there was confused about why I would shift to a management position. They thought I had so much money. After all, I was crushing it, wasn't I? Perhaps. But I was also broke. I was behind on my taxes. I was deep in credit card debt. If I'd tried to buy anything at all, the charges wouldn't have gone through. I was supporting my mom and my siblings. I was always in the red. As soon as the money came in, it went right back out. I took this job to be able to survive. Nobody knew the truth, and at that moment, I felt suffocated by it. I only hoped that as a leader, I could teach my agents to do as I said and not as I did. I hoped I could teach them the financial lessons I had learned the hard way.

If you're reading this and you don't work in real estate, you may be confused as to why I made $740,000 in income and was flat broke, even with all of my financial obligations to my family and everything

I paid in taxes. Well, in real estate, to make money, you have to spend money. Have you ever heard about how music artists who are signed to a record label can make a bunch of money and end up broke because they have to pay everyone else before they get paid? Well, it was kind of like that. The $740,000 was before I paid my split. So, as agreed, Keller Williams took a portion of the money as well as an office fee, which was what I paid to have a physical office to conduct business and meet with clients. Both of these expenses are standard at all traditional brokerages. And Keller Williams had a "capping" model that capped everyone's share of commission, a system far more generous than other brokerages. After that, I had to pay for coaching (which is not cheap). I also paid for much-needed assistants because the kind of volume I had to do to make that kind of income was not a one-man job. I had to pay for postcards, flyers, print ads, and everything else required to market each property. Those things came out of my pocket, not my clients'. I paid for lunches, dinners, drinks, and gifts for potential clients to score their business.

When everything was said and done, after paying all those people and spending all that money, I was taking home very, *very* little. Everything left over was divided among my family and me. I was living way beyond my means and spending as if I were actually bringing in $740,000 a year. I needed to find a way to bring in more. It was the only way I could keep my head above water. Fortunately, an opportunity came knocking around the same time I was starting my manager position.

I got a call from a representative of Countrywide with whom I often worked. "We noticed that you, as a company, have given us over forty million dollars in loan funding." I found it confusing, I wasn't a company—I was just an agent, and I knew I hadn't given them over $40 million in funding. It was half that at best. By loan fundings, they meant the total amount of money in the mortgages my clients had taken out. So, for example, if I had two clients who each took out mortgages for $250,000, I would have sent them $500,000 in loan fundings. As we continued our discussion, I started to understand more about how they had arrived at their $40 million figure. When I sell a home, I require a buyer to cross-qualify before I accept their offer. A preapproval is industry standard and a great way for a buyer to provide confidence that they will likely be approved for a loan. However, people can get preapprovals from all sorts of lenders. They can get a preapproval from their grandma, who is a "lender." It doesn't necessarily mean they will be approved for the loan. Believe me—I have been burned in the past.

Cross-qualification ensured a potential buyer would qualify with a lender whose standards I knew and trusted, regardless of whether they chose to go with that lender. A deal can fall through for many reasons, but I never want a deal to fall through because a buyer couldn't afford to purchase the home in the first place. It's a supreme waste of my sellers' time, and for every deal that fell through, we lost weeks if not months of market time during which a property could have gone to someone who *could* buy it. Anyway, every time my Countrywide representative cross-qualified a borrower, even when a buyer didn't end up purchasing the property, they would assign that client to me because I had referred them. If the buyer ended up using Countrywide later on, they added that amount to the funding amount I had sent them even if they didn't buy the property I was selling.

So, even though we had cleared up my initial confusion regarding the number of fundings, I was still unclear why he was calling. This was a lot of effort to simply thank me for something I had been unaware of in the first place.

"As an appreciation for the business you've brought us, we wanted to know if you would be interested in selling our REOs? Do you have experience with REOs?" he asked.

"Oh, of course, absolutely! I have plenty of experience with REOs," I responded without missing a beat.

Meanwhile, as we chatted on the phone, I was on Yahoo search-ing "what is an REO." I had absolutely no clue. It meant "Real Estate Owned" and was a fancy term for foreclosures. From then on, I was in the foreclosure business. My first one was in Encino, and it turned out to be the first of many. Selling REOs was very different than sell-ing a regular property. It required me to learn a completely new set of skills. I learned about "Cash for Keys," the eviction process, occu-pancy statuses, and price opinions. Every week, I would start with new properties in my dashboard, ready to begin the selling process. A lot of other agents viewed selling REOs as a headache. The more I heard my peer's opposition to selling REOs, the more opportunity I saw to carve out a little niche for myself. It paid off big-time.

◇◇◇

Finding financial stability required me to take risks and step outside my comfort zone. What made sense for me didn't necessarily make sense for others or even appeal to them. But I had to be honest with myself about my needs. Taking on new opportunities is something I seldom shy away from. If it's an opportunity other people aren't interested in, it makes me even more inter-ested. If you do what everyone else is doing, you will have a piece of what everyone else has. The more people there are doing the same thing, the smaller the piece. If you do what others do not do, you can have what they do not have. Which can be a good thing.

24. Becoming a Leader

*Before you speak, have a sip of shut the **** up water.*

GETTING THE HANG of my new position as a manager took some time, and initially, it wasn't without its hiccups. Recruiting agents was one of the most significant parts of my job. The first call I ever made to a potential recruit didn't go as well as I would have hoped. I had a list of all the agents in a particular brokerage with their phone numbers, and I planned to call each of them. I was sure at least one of them would be interested in taking a meeting. I started with the first name, dialed him up, and nervously waited. He answered! I started my pitch.

"Hi, my name is Harma, and I am with Keller Williams. I see your production is very impressive. Congratulations! Here at Keller Williams, we have amazing systems and models that we use to help our agents grow their business and maximize their potential. Would you be interested in learning more about what I can do to help you grow your business?"

"Are you sure you saw my production? Do you know who I am?" he asked confusedly on the other end.

"Yes, of course," I said while rereading his name.

"Here is what I want you to do. I want you to hang up the phone and find out who I am and then call me back." He hung up abruptly.

So I did a little research. I asked around and looked to see what I could find on the internet. It turns out his production was even better than I thought. He owned seven offices and was one of the most successful and well-respected brokers in the city. Imagine calling one of the most successful people in the industry you work in and offering them advice, unsolicited, on being better at their job. It was incredibly embarrassing, and most people wouldn't have called back. But I'm not most people. I dialed him up again.

"Hello again, it's Harma Hartouni with Keller Williams. I did my research. Congratulations on your success! I see you have multiple offices and have done very well for yourself," I said in my most chipper voice.

"Thank you." He responded with only slightly less confusion than he had in our initial conversation.

"I am wondering with our systems and models how we could help to grow your business even further if you were to merge with us. Would you be interested in learning more about what we at Keller Williams can do to grow your business?"

"You're a funny man. I admire your tenacity. You will go somewhere in life," he said, laughing.

"So . . . that's a no?" I asked.

"Yes, that's a no." He hung up.

If you haven't picked up on it by now, the word *no* never meant much to me. I always thought of a no as more of a *not yet*. I like to wear people down. More often than not, it's an effective tactic. Think about it: Have you ever gone to a shoe store and a salesperson immediately greets you and asks whether you need help and you instinctively say no then proceed to look for shoes the salesperson could have probably helped you find much faster? Perhaps when they come back, you are willing to say yes to their offer for help. Initial reactions can be overcome.

I worked very hard to recruit as many people as I could to our office. The challenge in recruitment was that often when I recruited someone, it was at a time when the market was going down. After all, though we had a superior product and resources at Keller Williams that incentivized a move, most people were most interested in making a move when they were hopeful for an upswing in their business. I was doing great business with foreclosures. But if the foreclosure market is hot, that means the general market is not. This presented an especially challenging situation because we desperately needed a better office. We had the ugliest office in the Valley. We couldn't compete with other brokerages if we didn't look like other brokerages. The owners wouldn't consider a new office until I had recruited one hundred agents. Keep in mind, for every agent you successfully recruit, you have to take exponentially more meetings, phone calls, and lunches. Only a fraction of those materialize into an actual hire.

Even with its challenges, I loved what I did. I loved being a leader. It gave me an opportunity to have a real, measurable impact on the success of many. When I took meetings, I felt empowered. I talked to recruits about my experience as an agent, my path, my success with REOs. It felt really good to talk about myself. Six months in, I realized I wasn't recruiting anybody. Nobody wanted to join my team, and I couldn't understand why. I decided to call my former manager, the man who recruited me to Keller Williams over sushi. I called him up and told him how, with every recruit, I followed the same script. We talked about the history of Keller Williams, the Keller Williams model, Keller Williams fees, splits, profit share, team building, then culture, then I tell them about myself, then my team, then the market, marketing, culture, and finally, my partner. Then the meeting is finished, they leave, and I never hear from them again.

His immediate response was an analogy. He said Keller Williams is like a diner's menu. When you go to a diner, there are so many options, and you can't possibly consider them all. You aren't going to sit and listen to a waitress explain every single thing on the menu—chicken sandwiches, pancakes, chili cheese fries, hot dogs, and milkshakes— it was all too much. You would feel completely overwhelmed and have no clue what to focus on. Instead, the waitress is going to listen to you and what interests you. That was how I needed to think about recruiting. I needed to let the recruit do the talking and listen to what interested them.

He told me to try something. Pour a glass of water and leave it on my desk. The water couldn't be replaced; it had to be the same glass of water, whether it was there for a month or six months. I was to consider that water *shut the fuck up water.* Anytime I wanted to monopolize the conversation or talk about myself, I had to take a drink of that water. Otherwise, if I didn't want to drink water that had been sitting on my desk for six months, all I needed to do was shut the fuck up and listen. So that's what I did. I found people wanted to connect by talking about themselves and feeling like someone cared and was actually listening to them.

It wasn't until my third year as a team leader that I hit the goal the owners had set for me. In that year, I recruited 101 agents. The recruitment record for Keller Williams, which had happened the year before, was sixty-seven agents. Nobody had ever recruited more than that in one year. I was determined to be number one. However, though I had recruited the most agents during the year, I was still ranked as number four, with three other team leaders ahead of me. It was a disappointment.

Once again, the time rolled around for the annual Keller Williams awards ceremony. This time it was in New Orleans. They finally got to the award for the best team leaders in the country. The awards were ranked. Fully expecting to be fourth, I braced myself for the announcement and subsequent disappointment. They began. Fifth place . . . fourth place . . . they didn't call my name. I wondered if my ranking had dropped even further. Third place . . . second place, and finally, the announcer called out, "The number-one team leader in the nation with a gross of one hundred forty-four agents recruited and a net of one hundred one agents recruited, the most in the history of

Keller Williams . . . Harma Hartouni!" As I walked across the stage in complete shock, Mark Willis, the CEO at the time, handed me my award. I was twenty-eight years old. I had been a team leader for three years. This was a huge accomplishment. After the awards ceremony, I cordially acknowledged the original owner who turned me down for the role of a manager. I couldn't help but think, *I bet you wish you had hired me now.*

I also went to one of the owners of my office and thanked her for taking a risk on me. That moment was career changing. It not only put me on the map, but it was validation I was truly good at what I did, better than everyone else that year. And it was confirmation of that same fact to my peers and leadership after several owners had turned me down for one reason or another. My English wasn't good enough. I was too gay for their office. I was too young for their office, etc. I had proven them all wrong. It felt so good. I felt powerful. I felt famous. I whispered to my assistant, "This must be how Madonna feels."

After congratulating me, my longtime coach made a point to remind me it wasn't about being number one. Rather, it was about being in the top five every single year. Consistency was the only way to build longevity. I knew the likelihood of being number one in recruiting a second year in a row was slim. After all, you can't recruit the entire world. Instead, I set my sights on being number one in profit. Sure enough, when the next year's awards came around, we were ranked as number one in profit share for all offices in their "launch phase." We *were* growing. I was growing. Year after year, the office grew and achieved new levels of success.

◇◇◇

The lesson my former manager taught me when I called him up for guidance is one of the most important lessons any leader can learn. Regardless of what you do, if you work with people, you must be a good listener. In my experience, so many people are open books. They will tell you everything you need to know to help them succeed and, in turn, help you succeed. But they want to feel heard, genuinely heard. It doesn't matter how much experience you have or how successful you have been at what you do. If you can't make others feel heard, then you can't be a good leader. People don't care how much you know until they know how much you care.

25. Building a Team

One hundred percent of nothing is nothing.

With my success as a team leader, opportunities for ownership started to come my way. I knew I didn't want to be a team leader forever, and my eventual goal was to be an owner. It was just a matter of when. I was still getting an enormous amount of fulfillment in my role and felt a great deal of pride in my team. I was not sure whether I was ready to leave just yet. I was finally in the green with my real estate transactions and still very much focused on my niche market of REOs. I was putting my team leader's salary back into the business in one way or another. If an agent was struggling financially, I would pay for their dues, food, sometimes even rent. I paid for agents to attend conventions they couldn't afford out of pocket. I would use some of my salary to give bonuses in the first few years before we were solvent. When we moved to a new office, I paid for our new signage. To save money and decrease our overhead, I cut our cleaning crew. But I didn't tell the team. If they knew we were cutting costs, they might worry about the financial state of the office. We were doing well but still in a period of growth, and cost-cutting was an effective way of ensuring we could continue to invest in that growth. After everyone went home at night around 9:00 p.m., my number two, Meagan, and I took off our leadership hats and put on our cleaning hats (and gloves). We vacuumed, scrubbed the bathrooms, dusted, everything we could do to make it look like a cleaning crew had come. It saved us $1,200 a month, and we were able to put that money to good use. As the office's phantom janitor, one of the things that bothered me to no end was liquid in the wastebaskets. The curse words that came out of my mouth when an agent's stale coffee spilled all over me would make anyone blush. I decided to email the office and tell them that the "cleaning crew" had noticed a lot of liquids in the waste bins and asked that we empty them in the sink before trashing them going forward. It worked like a charm. Keeping everything secret from the office wasn't just about morale boosting, though that was a big part of it. It was also about defending ourselves against competitors. If our competition found out we were cutting costs to keep the lights on, they would descend upon my hard-gained team like vultures. I couldn't have that. We had wine and cheese events, happy hours, everything you would expect in a successful company's culture. Can you say fake it till you make it? It was my mantra.

The first holiday party we ever threw was at a small pizza place. It was all we could afford. We dined on pizza and breadsticks, and our entertainment for the night was an agent who played the piano. It was all we could afford, and a stark contrast to the other more established Keller Williams offices' holiday parties that were thrown at hotels and event centers with caterers and open bars. I had to do what I could to create a culture that people wanted to be a part of. That was what was most important to me. It was the only way to add value. My goal and my mission were always to attract agents with the value of what my office could offer them. It was never to attract agents purely with financial incentives.

Often, when recruiting agents, one of the first questions they asked was, "What is your split?" I always responded, "Why does it matter?" In my view, if I was building a culture and environment with resources that would inevitably help an agent to grow their business and, as a result, make more money, what difference did it make what my splits were as long as they were standard? I always focused on what I could offer them and how my office might be the right fit for them. I wanted it to be the right choice for both my office and the agent. I often invited recruits to our after-hours events. I wanted our culture to speak for itself, and I could count on my existing team members to be candid about their satisfaction with my leadership. Never appearing too eager, I took the position with every recruit that we should date before we got married. I'm not for everyone, and neither is my office.

On the same token, every recruit was not for us. I remember one particular recruit who came for an interview with me. She was Iranian, as well, and as soon as we sat down, she asked me whether I spoke Farsi. I lied and said no. I knew if we spoke in Farsi, she would want to negotiate fees and splits, and I don't negotiate. I told her I could explain a bit about our model and our company for about three minutes, being careful not to bore her, and then afterward, she could ask me to expound on anything that stuck out to her. She raised her hand in the air and waved it slowly, the way one would signify they were uninterested in what you had to say.

"I'm not interested in your story. I just want to know your commission split, and that's it," she said.

"Okay, well, what is your split now?" I asked with a hint of annoyance in my voice, knowing already this was never going to work out.

"I am on a one hundred percent split and I keep all my commission."

"OK, well, can I have your last name?"

She handed me her business card, and I immediately got on my computer and looked her up on a program we used to see other agents' production records. I looked to see how well she had done for the past year. She hadn't successfully closed a single deal. I looked up the past two years. Zero deals. Three years, four years. Zero deals. I turned to her.

"Do you think the fact that your office is shutting down has something to do with the fact you are on a one hundred percent split?" I asked her.

"The shutdown is not my problem. That is what my brokerage offered, and so I took it."

"Well, no business can stay open if they aren't getting paid. But that's beside the point. When you came in, you told me you were proud to see another Persian [aka Iranian] be so successful at such a young age. My goal is to continue being successful, and I can't do that by giving my agents one hundred percent splits. Here is what I will do. I will give you a one hundred percent split until you sell a property. Once you close on your first property, I will move you to seventy-thirty, where you would keep seventy percent of your commission. The next day, I will move you back to a one hundred percent split until you sell your next property. So, when you don't sell, you can tell yourself you have a one hundred percent split, and when you do sell, we will move you to seventy-thirty. How does that sound?"

"That makes absolutely no sense."

"I completely agree. I don't think we are a good match."

Angrily, she got up, and the meeting was over. As I saw her out of the office, I turned to her and wished her good luck . . . in Farsi. She was not a good fit because her only interest was how she could bene-fit; she had no interest in building a stronger team or being part of a successful whole. A 100 percent split sounds great, but she clearly wasn't getting the support or resources she needed to be an effective agent. So her awesome split was worthless. As a leader, I had a choice in who was a part of our organization. Since I started, it was my mission to create a culture. That was our value. I felt strongly that one bad apple could and would spoil the entire basket. I could afford to be selective when it truly mattered. For the sake of my team, I couldn't afford not to be.

My leadership style with my agents has always been to focus on their strengths. I think it is a uniquely American phenomenon to focus on weaknesses rather than strengths. Whereas where I come from, we tend to zero in on a person's strengths and build off that. For example, I was good at math, so that was what I focused on in school. Call me pessimistic, but I don't think anyone can ever be good at their weakness. Sure, they can improve. But what is there to say about all of the wasted energy trying to get better at something you were never that good at to begin with? When you are competing with someone good at that thing, whatever it may be, it's likely no matter how much you work on it, you won't be as good as the person it comes naturally to. Instead, I believe you should put that energy into being even better at your strengths.

I knew a family with a son who was extremely gifted in art but bad at math. The family forced him to study math every single day. They hired tutors, and he had a mandatory study time. They hammered math into his head. He had time for art only once a week, on Saturdays. Art became an escape, a novelty for a hard week's work. Eventually, his teacher told his parents he should focus more on his art; it was what he was good at and what he loved. He was never going to be good at math. I couldn't help but wonder why they were spending so much time and effort on something he will never dedicate his life to? He hates it!

I apply that logic to my leadership. If you have an agent who is terrible at cold-calling, they shouldn't be wasting their time trying to lead-generate on the phone. They should be out in the field meeting people face to face. On the flip side, if an agent is great on the phone but terrible in person, they shouldn't be forced to do open houses. I don't know any agent, including myself, who is good at it all.

Whenever meeting a potential recruit, I dug into them to get a better idea of how they spent their time. I asked things like: Who is your role model? What inspired you to get into real estate? How was your week or weekend? Who inspires you? Who did you shadow most recently? What book did you read most recently? I tried to get an idea of what their career was before they decided to make the jump into real estate, as often people transition into the industry from another. I asked everyone where they saw themselves in a year. Specifically, if we look forward one year and are celebrating their first year in real estate, what exactly are we celebrating? What does that look like? Eye contact is imperative; it helps people feel cared for and heard. Another tactic I used is to pay attention to words and anecdotes people used in conversations with me. At the end of the conversation, I found a way to bring up one or two of their own words and anecdotes as a way to show them I had both listened to and heard them. I made it my mission to make them feel comfortable, to understand them, to truly hear their stories. Some people are faster to share than others, and others need to ease into opening up. My goal was always to figure out a way to break down that wall. This was effective in figuring out what drove them and, eventually, what their purpose was. Good leaders know when you help others find their purpose, your world expands along with theirs.

I also tried very hard to get an idea of my recruits' and eventual team members' lives. I have never viewed this as overstepping. I view it as having a vested interest in my team members' lives because it has a direct effect on their performance. Home life and business life work in tandem with one another. If one is bad, the other will be affected in some way. If your business is going well and your home life is not, you can use your resources to reconnect with your partner through trips, therapy, taking up a hobby, etc. If your personal life is good but your business is not, you rely on that close personal support to motivate you and guide you through tough times. I became a therapist for many of my team members. In doing so, I learned more about their fears, their comforts and discomforts, and their goals. It helped me hold them accountable. I never recruited to Keller Williams; Keller Williams spoke for itself. It truly was the best model. I recruited to me. I was winning people over with my leadership and my genuine care for their success and well-being. That was the value. We had higher fees, our physical office was a shithole, and the location was far from the best. And yet my former manager in Studio City couldn't beat me. Not with split or a more beautiful office.

My emotional intelligence and intuition are two of the most important factors in my success. When someone lets me in and I connect with them, it helps me to understand their needs. It helps me to understand how they are going to approach a situation that assists in giving them the support best tailored to them. I pick up on eye contact; if someone is willing to look you in your eyes, it means they are willing to connect with you. If they don't look you in your eyes, they are closed off to you. Another factor in my success has been my low-stakes approach. I don't need someone else to help me win. That sounds a lot more conceited than it is. When I say that, I mean I don't need anything from someone else. If I intend to connect with someone to make them better at what they do, it comes from a legitimate desire to help them reach their potential because I care. It isn't because I want something from them. It's exhausting to make an effort not to care. It's easy to care. At the same time, it's even more exhausting to pretend to care. I won't pretend.

Everyone has some sort of story that has shaped where they are as a person, whether they realize it or not. I've spent plenty of time in therapy. Like, a lot of time. And during that time, I have finally become aware of the events in my life that have shaped not only who I am but my behaviors, my strengths, and my weaknesses. I'm sure just from reading this book, you can see a clear delineation between where I come from and who I am today. Some people aren't as self-aware . . . yet. After all, it took me years, and I am still learning about myself. Nonetheless, I have found that when people let me in and are willing to be open about their past and vulnerable with me, I can use that knowledge to figure out the best way to support them and even help them overcome whatever negative effects those experiences have had.

Another quality that I have attributed to my success and have tried to instill in my team members is the value of doing something important even if it makes you uncomfortable. Remember when I used to have to scrub the pool at the garden house? I did it before I did anything else, and it sucked. But when it was done, and I wouldn't have to do it again until we returned. I use that same energy in my business and that was further reinforced by reading the book *Eat That Frog* by Brian

Tracy. Think about it: the best way to lose weight is to eat less. It's not rocket science. If you want to lose weight, deep down, you probably know what you need to do. Adjust the way you eat. You cut out alcohol and sugar. You eat lettuce and chicken breasts with no dressing for each meal. It's terrible, but it works. Whatever your goals are, if you make tangible steps toward them and don't falter, you will probably reach them eventually.

Whenever we went to a convention, I made a point to make it fun for my team. We went out every night to bars and clubs and had an amazing time. It was perfect for building morale and letting off steam. I guess I was the troublesome team leader. The same year I was named the number-one team leader, Keller Williams had a panel discussion with all top-five team leaders during the annual convention. Well, the panel I was scheduled to be a part of started at 8:00 a.m. sharp. And it wasn't exactly the best idea to go out and get wasted in New Orleans the night before with my team. I was hungover.

I woke up at 7:15 a.m., and the convention center was about fifteen minutes away. I wasn't prepared. I had missed the rehearsal and had no idea what the questions were going to be. I got ready as fast as possible and ran to the convention center. My brain was already operating at about 50 percent, and the remaining space was filled with worry. How do I look older? I was insecure about looking too young in comparison to the other team leaders. How do I make sure my accent isn't too thick? Who is going to be there? I was a ball of anxiety.

When I arrived, the president of the educational department, the CEO, and other C-suite executives were all sitting in the very front row of the auditorium. They gave us microphones and pushed us out on the stage. I have zero doubt I looked like a deer caught in headlights. Speaking of headlights, the overhead lights were so blinding that even though there were about three thousand people there, I could see only the most important leaders in our company. I sat in a row with the rest of the team leaders, and the panel began. I was shaking.

Thank God, or how some Armenians like to say, "Thanks God," the first question went to the person sitting on the opposite end of the panel. They asked her simple, innocuous questions.

"Hi, where are you from? How long have you been a team leader? And how do you tackle recruiting and appointments?" the moderator asked.

"I wake up. I do affirmations because I am a positive thinker. I have a coach, and I love what I do. I am passionate about recruiting and appointments, and I love to connect with new people!"

She finished, and everyone clapped in a way that seemed primarily out of obligation. Lots of rays of sunshine, right? They moved on to the next person and asked the same questions. His responses were along the same lines. "I love what I do. I do my mediation when I wake up. I get to the office by seven thirty, and I lead generate until noon. I love to do it!"

The third person went. "I love my job. Recruiting is my life. I delegate everything to everyone else. I am always on the phone and recruiting!" he announced with excitement.

The fourth panelist spoke and said the same crap. I got worried. I knew if I focused too hard on saying something similar, which would be lies, I would be able to speak English properly. If I said what I wanted to say, I wouldn't have to worry about my English, but people may not have liked what I had to say. The mic came to me. I was sitting in one of those high chairs they always put panelists in to make them look authoritative. I crouched down a bit; my right leg was bent at the knee with my foot resting on my other knee. It was the manliest stance I could think of and also the most uncomfortable. I collected my thoughts and told myself to get it together.

I could not mess this up. I tried to wish away my hangover. I held the mic up to my mouth, looked at the other panelists, and said what I thought. "I admire you all, and I am sorry that I don't know you. I didn't show up to the practice. I love how you all wake up and love to lead generate and feel so passionate about it. I don't know if I am on the wrong panel, but I personally don't like lead generation. As a matter of fact, I hate it. It's just not my favorite part of the day." The back of the auditorium began to laugh inappropriately. The front row looked confused and pissed off. The woman leading the panel looked at me, and I swear her eyes were red with anger.

"So, you don't like lead generation, and you don't like to be on the phone?" she asked.

"That is correct. I do not," I said truthfully.

"That's interesting because you recruited more than double the number of people as the person sitting next to you. How did you do this if you hate cold-calling and lead generation?" Her tone was somewhere between genuinely curious and still pissed off.

"Oh, I cold-called," I said.

"You just said you didn't."

"I never said I didn't. I just said I hate it. I honestly don't see how you guys love it. If you want to have a six-pack and you eat lettuce and chicken breast every single day, you can get a six-pack, but it doesn't mean you learn to love the chicken breast and lettuce. I wanted to be number one, so all I did was cold-call. I knew how many I needed to hit my goal, and once I did, I practically threw the phone to the other side of the room. Every time I made a call with a prospect, I meditated too. My meditation was: *This person is going to join. This person is going to join. This person is going to join.* I knew if they joined, I wouldn't have to get on the phone again."

People laughed and cheered until I finished speaking. After the panel was over, agent after agent came up to commend me for being honest. I told them I just couldn't lie. Who likes cold-calling? You call someone, they say, "Fuck you. Don't call me again," and you smile and say, "Have a nice day," eager to call the next person? Give me a break!

◇ ◇ ◇

You don't have to learn to love the things you hate, even if you have to do them. Look at the things you dislike for what they are—a means to an end. Prioritize them, do them first, and get them out of the way so you can move on. Save the best for last and worst for first. You'll be better off for it.

26. Operating Principal at Last

I had so many issues until I realized I was the issue.

As THINGS IN MY PROFESSIONAL LIFE were moving full steam ahead, my personal life with my partner was following suit. We were finally out of debt, and both our careers were in an upswing. I was a successful team leader, and my team was closing over one hundred transactions per year. It was time to take the next step. And what better way than to buy a new home.

It wasn't our first home together, it was our third, but it represented a shift in our reality and, in many ways, a celebration of hard work and success. It was a charming 1930s bungalow in the Valley. As lovely as the home was, we weren't exactly 1930s bungalow kind of people. Never ones to do things easily, as soon as we bought the house, we tore it down. The intention was to construct a completely modern home from the ground up. A lot of people assumed we were doing this because, for a real estate professional like me, building a house and the typical headaches that come along with it would be much easier to navigate. False! My expertise was in selling homes, not building them. The idea that I would be knowledgeable about new construction is equivalent to a car salesman being knowledgeable about how to engineer a Tesla. What ensued was chaos.

The architect we hired was simply too new and green to be able to oversee it properly. He made mistake after mistake. Our deadlines were pushed and pushed. And eventually, there was no other choice than for me to step in and help oversee the project. I know HGTV makes these kinds of projects seem like a breeze, even fun! Reality shows are not always reality.

Building this home was a nightmare. Every day I ran back and forth from work to the construction site, the construction site to our apartment, around and around I went. It took a total of nine months. But it felt like years. My partner and I almost broke up three separate times. Who knows how much money I lost in my business by focusing so much on the house and not on my work. I remember my first broker turning down the opportunity to sell that multimillion-dollar home in Glendale. He did it because he knew working outside his expertise would require more of him than working within his expertise would.

Every time your focus is not on your expertise, you are going to lose money. It's an opportunity cost issue. In that instance, the opportunity cost didn't balance. Similarly, the opportunity to build our own home was not worth the effort. It was a valuable lesson. Building is fun when it isn't your house. But for my family and the sake of my marriage, I will NEVER build another home from the ground up. I don't care if I am a billionaire. I will find a house that is already constructed and move right in.

After we moved into our new home, our lives continued to push forward. My partner was on the fast track at his company. It seemed he was being promoted year after year. Never having to ask or apply for a new position, his work ethic spoke for itself, and he was on everyone's radar all the way to the C-suite. It was an immensely proud day for both of us when he called me up and told me that he had been promoted to a vice president within a new division. I cried with excitement. After everything we had been through, living in a tiny apartment, maxing out credit cards and paying off one another's debts, struggling to make ends meet, and eating ramen when there was nothing else. It was a full-circle moment—for both of us. I felt just as invested in his success as he had been in mine when he bought me my real estate books so many years before. At that moment, I decided that it was finally time for me to own my own real estate office. He had inspired me.

Owning my own real estate office had been a longstanding goal of mine; it was just a matter of when. I felt comfortable with the impact I had made as a team leader and felt strongly that I had proven myself. After all, when I became a team leader, our office was making no money whatsoever. In the time I had been running the office, we had almost quadrupled our number of agents and were one of the most success-ful offices in the country. We did all of that when the market was in a complete downturn from 2007 to 2010. We were able to grow when the housing market was in freefall. As Gary Keller, the founder of Keller Williams, says, "Volume follows numbers." During this process, I learned the more I recruited, the more likely it was that we would grow. He was right.

Within a week of my partner's promotion, I scheduled a meeting with the owners of my office. Becoming an owner had been discussed before. A stake in the company had been promised to me whenever I was ready for it. I went into the meeting, excited to reveal to them that I was finally ready to take that step. Their response was not what I was expecting. They said I wasn't ready. Actually, no. They said I hadn't earned it. I think that was even worse. I was the reason their office was solvent. It was my hard work and tenacity that had made it what it was. I would venture to say I had more ownership and was more invested in the success of the office than any of them had ever been. And yet, when the opportunity came to put their money where their mouths were, the fruits of my efforts were undervalued.

I knew it was time to leave. I couldn't stay in an environment where I wasn't valued, and I also couldn't delay my success to appease other people's monetary interests. Most importantly, I couldn't stay somewhere I was unhappy. Staying together for the sake of the kids would only drive them away. I knew that if I stayed, the culture I had built would start to deteriorate, and my agents would start to leave.

Fortunately, as I was making my departure, a fantastic opportunity came up for me to purchase a stake in Keller Williams Calabasas and become the operating principal. The infamous office that hadn't come to fruition when I was looking for a manager role eventually did open, and it was available. I jumped at the opportunity and finally had an ownership stake. The office was small, there were only nine agents, and they had very little market share. But I knew I could help them grow. Sure enough, eventually, we had over a hundred agents and the second-largest market share in the area.

As operating principal, I was in a much different position than I had been as a team leader. I wasn't managing the day-to-day of my office anymore. I had to entrust that responsibility to others. It wasn't easy. I hired and fired manager after manager. After I let the fifth manager go, I was driving home complaining about them to a friend when it hit me. The managers weren't the problem; I was the problem. Think about it: if you are driving around town and everywhere you turn someone is about to hit your car, and you find yourself cursing them and getting angry with them, you may want to pull over and consider whether your driving is the problem.

As a team lead, I learned as I went and did absolutely everything I could to build the office I led from the ground up. I stayed late every night, spent my own money for the betterment of my team, and truly gave everything I had to create something amazing. After building our agent count and market share, Keller Williams Calabasas was doing really, *really* well. I thought it was a manager's dream scenario, everything was already built, and all they had to do was come in and manage it. I realized that I was looking at each manager and comparing them to me, the scrappy hungry me who fought tooth and nail to keep the lights on as a team leader.

To be honest, I viewed each manager hire as lazy. When they said they were working from home, I wondered, *For what? We aren't IBM consultants.* When they said they were leaving at 5:00 p.m., I asked, "Have you set up enough appointments for tomorrow?" When a manager said he needed more space when we already had an eight-thousand-square-foot office, I couldn't help but remember the tiny little dank space that I made work. But comparing the managers to me was the wrong way to view their impact. Not because I thought no one could compare to me but because I was hiring managers who were experienced in environments that didn't operate like mine.

I had created this unique culture, and it was an essential part of what I had built. I decided then and there that the next manager I hired would be someone I could groom and mentor to operate the way we did things. Now, when I hire a manager, I have three pages of the line-by-line expectations for new hires. I want it to be clear on the outset that we operate differently than other brokerage offices. It is the best way to ensure the culture is maintained. As a leader, for the sake of your team, you have to be responsible for where you are and where you are going. I have never been shy about being extremely intentional in shaping environments in the way I think they will operate best and expecting the people under me to follow suit. It has served me well so far.

One of the regional partners of the Calabasas office also owned a piece of an office in Studio City. After seeing the success of the Calabasas office, he approached me and asked whether I would be interested in becoming the operating principal of the Studio City office. Studio City was where I had begun my real estate career at Keller Williams. It was a treat to be able to go back as an owner. Soon after, an opportunity came to become the operating principal of the Encino and Sherman Oaks office, the office that had turned me down when I originally expressed interest in purchasing. The office that I had led from the dust and into success. Once again, I jumped at the

opportunity. Eventually, I was the operating principal of three separate Keller Williams offices, two of which I had already worked for.

In 2017, as operating principal of three Keller Williams offices, we
achieved over $2.5 billion in volume with nearly nine hundred agents.
Being the operating principal of three offices was a dream come true,
but I decided I wanted to focus on one office that was completely mine. I
sold my shares of Calabasas and Studio City and became the sole owner
of the Sherman Oaks/Encino office. In our first year, we closed over
thirteen hundred transactions and did about $1.3 billion in volume.

*Unexpectedly, when I had legitimate ownership of my offices, I was faced
with a challenge many leaders face. Particularly leaders who have built up
something far beyond where it had ever been before. I found it challenging to
cede control. By this time, my success spoke for itself, and as a result, it made
me feel like my way of doing things, in my office, was the best way. All it
did was make me resent the efforts of my team members. I had to learn that
others deserve an opportunity to learn from their experiences, just as I did.
I could not expect them to act the same way or approach things as I would.
We can teach from experience, but we can't teach experience.*

27. Starting a Family

I BELIEVE one of the most challenging things anyone can do is build something they have never seen before. Some people are better at it than others; Elon Musk dreams up rocket ships at night and builds them the next day. But for most people, creating something for which you have no model, formula, or example of isn't just hard—it is downright daunting.

With our careers firmly in place, my partner and I were finally able to sit back and enjoy and breathe. We were still grinding, but not in the ways we had for so many years. We had a foundation, we had a sense of security, and we felt comfort in what seemed to be the trajectory for our lives. Two successful people making good money whose only responsibilities were to themselves. Now, obviously, we had responsibilities to our loved ones, but they were voluntary responsibilities. When we went home at night, it was about us and nobody else.

Our first vacation together.

Our lifestyle was one where we could easily go out to a bar on a weeknight or meet up for dinner spontaneously. We could see a movie at a moment's notice or even take an extended getaway. And one weekend, we did just that. We jumped in our car and drove down to Palm Springs.

It's about two hours from Los Angeles, just short enough to feel manageable and long enough to feel like a real trip. As we drove, my phone rang, and it was my sister. She was bubbling with excitement, and I could tell in her voice that she was grinning from ear to ear. She wanted to give us the great news—she was expecting a baby!

My first reaction was sheer happiness for her and her new husband. It would be my first niece or nephew, and adding a child to our family was sure to bring a newfound sense of joy. But I also had mixed emotions. It felt a little bizarre. It's always odd to see a sibling, especially a younger one, move to a new stage of life. Particularly such a significant one. It felt like just yesterday I was conspiring to bring her to the US as her guardian. Now she was married and having a baby. Time was moving, and life was changing quickly.

Once we arrived, we checked into our hotel, freshened up, and then headed to a nice dinner. As we sat enjoying our meal, my mind was elsewhere. I was completely silent, with my mind racing trying to make sense of my confused emotions. I looked around, surveying the room and realizing that what I saw could very well be our future. If you aren't familiar with Palm Springs, you should know that it is a gay hotspot with a lot of gay men from the surrounding cities like LA. The room was filled with gay men. Many were older and clearly successful, having a lovely weekend getaway just like us. My partner asked whether we should consider buying a property in Palm Springs one day. Strange timing.

No caption needed.

I thought, *If we buy property here, who will I leave it to? Who am I going to leave anything to? Am I destined to be the rich gay uncle who swoops in at holidays and birthdays with fabulous gifts and a trip to Europe at graduation?* It didn't excite me at all. As much as I loved my partner, I wasn't sure whether I wanted it to just be the two of us for the rest of our lives. We were ambitious, and we were successful; our careers were a huge part of our lives. But was that how it would always be? So many years ago, when I envisioned my life, I imagined it with an Armenian wife and children. Had I lost that part of me?

I looked at my partner from across the table and blurted out, "I want to have kids!"

He looked back at me, surprised. "You never wanted kids before."

"I know. But what do we really want? Do we want to be old and only have our travels and our home to show for our life together? I don't want that. Just because we are gay doesn't mean we can't have a family," I said.

"I think we should," he agreed, surprisingly painlessly.

"Are you sure?"

"Yes, let's do it."

One of my best qualities is I never take too much time thinking over decisions. I like to go with my gut. I move quickly. On the flip side, one of my worst qualities is once I have decided I want something, I can't rest until I have it. I can't forget possibilities or unimagine goals. My brain just doesn't work that way. Once we decided to have kids, there was no stopping the process.

As soon as we returned to LA, I started researching surrogate and donor agencies. I set up interviews with as many as I could find. We met with birth mothers, learned about the process, and set aside money in a trust. It took about two years to save enough money. Surrogacy is extremely expensive. The decision to go with a surrogate instead of adoption was simply because of how difficult it was for gay couples to adopt. I heard difficult stories of birth mothers changing their minds or relatives coming out of the woodwork demanding money. I couldn't imagine how difficult that might be. I felt surrogacy would give us the most control over the process. I took comfort in the idea the surrogate would not be biologically related to the child and a legal process was in place with a separate egg donor. While it doesn't necessarily sound warm and fuzzy, it was important to me that we knew no one could ever take our child away from us. Once we had saved enough money, everything started to move so quickly. Hadn't we just decided to have kids over dinner in Palm Springs? But then, perhaps *decided* isn't the right term. It wasn't necessarily that I had made the decision but that I had allowed myself to accept children as a possibility.

No matter how we sliced it, this was immensely uncharted territory. We did not have a model for building a family like this. I had pictured myself as a father so many times, so long ago in Iran. But back then, I saw it through that lens. I saw myself married to a woman, having a baby the old-fashioned way. After I moved to the US, accepted that I was gay, and came out of the closet, I put the idea of having children out of my head. Of course, I would never have children. It just didn't seem possible. And yet here we were, starting the process of surrogacy.

I was almost thirty-three when our first child, our son, was born. It was beautiful and scary, exciting and surreal. A year later, we decided to try for a girl, the idea being that we wanted two children, one of each. Our doctor recommended we implant both of our remaining embryos to give us the highest chance of one taking. And sure enough, they both took. Our twin girls were born when I was thirty-four.

The biggest challenge with parenting for me was we were literally creating something we had not seen before. Not just because we were gay parents; there were other gay families we had met in LA. We were Middle Eastern gay parents. We belonged to a culture that did not believe gay existed and certainly did not believe two men could raise a child. I knew as our children got older and learned about who they were, there would always be an inherent discord between their heritage and their family structure. It was just the way it was.

I also had never seen a healthy, functional family firsthand. I did not grow up in one. I had to be a dad, a good dad. I refused to be anything but a good father. But when you come from a dysfunctional situation like mine, the fear of fucking up your kids or repeating your own parents' mistakes is always in the back of your mind. Ultimately, I just had to have faith. My partner and I did not have children by accident. We didn't have them because we felt like it was the natural next step or what everyone expected—quite the contrary. We had children because we absolutely wanted them and knew our lives would not feel complete until we had them. At the end of the day, I had to let go of the fear and hope for the best.

Now, almost six years later, with children who are school-aged, I feel more confident in my parenting. So confident, I even give people parenting advice. If anyone ever asks me, my parenting advice is simple. Kids need love, so love them. If every decision you make is derived from your desire to provide them the love they crave, the decisions that come afterward feel much more intuitive and the mistakes you make, much more forgivable. I don't believe children need to be showered with love all day. That's a standard that will likely be too hard to keep up as a parent, and it will not do your children any favors as they get older and start to leave the nest. Instead, I believe children need pure love and to know that they are loved unconditionally. No matter what.

◇◇◇

Life is a curious thing. For me, it is hard not to feel a world away from where my life began almost forty years ago. I mean, technically, I am a world away from Iran. But it's not just about geography. I grew up in a place where I was not meant to exist—a place where my identity was contrary to culture, standards, and faith. I grew up in a home filled with dysfunction and strife, with a parent who struggled to provide the love and security someone like me so desperately needed. I carried the weight of all of that on my shoulders as early as I was able to perceive it. A weight that made me feel unworthy, afraid, and alone. But if you carry a weight constantly, eventually you become stronger.

I resigned myself to live a life that was not necessarily based on who I was or what I wanted but on what was expected of me, finding happiness in the shadows and never fully coming into the light. But then everything changed on that fateful day, on the side of a mountain. Unbeknownst to me, the weight I carried and the strength I built was all so I could fight. I fought to walk again, I fought to come to the US, I fought for success, and I fought for the privilege to live my life in truth. I fought for love and for family. When I was lying on the road, in shock with my legs mangled, I didn't know it, but I was just beginning a fight for my life—a life of happiness, hard-earned and well-deserved happiness.

My father eventually moved to the US permanently, and he and my mother divorced. He lives in LA, and we have a relationship. I make sure he has what he needs, and I don't harbor resentment toward him anymore. My mother is happier than she has ever been. It took some time, but when she started to open her eyes to the love my partner and I have for one another, she found her way toward acceptance. She struggled with my sexuality for many reasons, but the biggest one was because she loved me. And if there is genuine love from parent to child, a parent will eventually find a way to love that child for who they are.

It's funny—the hills in LA sometimes remind me of the hills in Bumehen where our garden house was. That house was meant to be a source of pride for the life my father built. I can't help but feel the same sense of pride for my own home. I feel it when I get home and my cocker spaniels come and greet me to say hello. I feel it when my mom is over and I hear her and my aunt making coffee in my kitchen, laughing, feeling right at home. I feel it when I walk past my family room and see my husband, asleep after a long day, and our kids watching a movie snuggled next to him. I feel it when I go to sleep, knowing everyone under my roof is happy, healthy, and loved unconditionally.

I guess if pride is what having a garden house is all about, I sort of have my own. But, just in case you were wondering, someone else cleans the pool.

Acknowledgments

The journey of this book had many passengers, and I want to share my love and appreciation for my partner who never says no to any adventure, allows me to be me, and accepts me the way I am. Thank you, Asad. I would like to thank Jon Fox, who not only helped me create this book but listened carefully, helped me put my thoughts and memory on paper, and was my biographer on this journey. I would like to acknowledge my sister, brother, and mother for their love and support, and my father, who helped shape who I am today. I would also like to acknowledge the leadership of my company and our agents, who have shaped my life by giving me the opportunity to be in business with them and who have trusted me, made a decision to be with me, and show me unconditional love. I wouldn't be where I am without you.

About the Author

Harma Hartouni is a self-made entrepreneur and developer, owns a real estate company employing hundreds of residential and commercial real estate agents in Southern California, and runs the #1-ranked real estate business in his region. Harma has created a successful brand with his growing business footprint in Los Angeles, building a large real estate practice exceeding $1 billion in sales in 2019. As founder and CEO of multiple companies serving the local real estate market, Harma's businesses include financial services, technology, and coaching—a personal passion Harma has developed in to advising some of the top agents in the country on strategies to grow their businesses.

Harma creates real estate portfolios for investors, runs a highly profitable escrow company, and has expanded into property development with multiple active projects. Among awards and recognition received, the National Association of Realtors named Harma one of their top "30 Under 30" brokers in the country, and the *Los Angeles Business Journal* has recognized him as one of their "40 Under 40" Most Influential Business Owners.

Harma lives in Los Angeles with his partner, their three children, three dogs, and two turtles.

9 781736 241608